SYSTEM CRASH

An activist guide to making revolution

By Neil Faulkner, Phil Hearse, Nina Fortune,
Rowan Fortune, and Simon Hannah

Published by Resistance Books, London
International Institute for Research and Education, Amsterdam

© Neil Faulkner, Phil Hearse, Nina Fortune,
    Rowan Fortune, and Simon Hannah

ISBN 978-0-902869-50-9

Published February 2021
by Resistance Books, London
International Institute for Research and Education, Amsterdam

System Crash is issue no. 70 of the IIRE Notebooks for Study and Research.

Design and typeset by Adam Di Chiara

Contents

Introduction

World on Fire

We may be alone in the universe. Despite ever better technology for look-ing and listening in space, we have still found no evidence for intelligent life elsewhere. Equally significant, as far as we know, no other life-form has ever attempted to make contact with us. Our species, homo sapiens, may be an accident, a chance event, a mere blip in an eternity of time and space otherwise devoid of intelligent life.

Either way, what now seems certain is that our species is hurtling towards extinction; or, at the very least, towards a comprehensive break-down of existing civilisation, a collapse into some sort of post-apocalyp-tic dystopia. This is not science-fiction: it is extrapolation based on the current trajectory of global society; it is a statement about the depth of the world capitalist crisis of the early 21st century.

That this is the worst crisis in human history is now beyond reasonable doubt. There are three main reasons for this.

First, the rulers of the world control arsenals of weapons capable of destroying every living thing on the planet. In the First World War, they killed 15 million. In the Second World War, they killed 60 million. In a Third World War, they could kill everyone.

Anyone who thinks that because of the possible consequences this could never happen is a fool. The historian Eric Hobsbawm described the 20th century – with its wars, genocides, and hecatombs of dead – as 'the Age of Extremes'. We have moved on. We now surely live in 'the Age of Madness' – an age when imbeciles, narcissists, and psychopaths are given control over thousands of nuclear missiles.

Perhaps we will avoid nuclear Armageddon. We cannot, however, on present trajectories, avoid climate catastrophe, ecological devastation, and recurring pandemics.

Our rulers are committed to a system based on profit, corporate power, and exponential growth – a system of unlimited capital accumulation that has now burst the limits of sustainability and begun to destroy the planet's ecology. No-one can escape the consequences. This is the second reason for thinking this to be history's greatest crisis.

Here is the third. In the past, hundreds of millions lived as farmers in remote countryside providing for their own subsistence; they were not impacted by the hunger of the Great Depression, the carnage of the Second World War, the fears of the Cold War.

Today, the traditional peasantry has largely disappeared, absorbed into the agribusiness complexes and mega-cities of capitalism's final frontier. The pandemic, climate change, war, economic stagnation, social collapse, creeping fascism, police repression: the whole of humanity is engulfed by this compound crisis of the world system.

There is a way out, but it will not be easy. No amount of tinkering, no programme of piecemeal reform will do. It is not a matter replacing a leader, electing a new party, or changing the voting system. The political structures embedded in the system – let us give it a name: neoliberal capitalism; or globalised, financialised, monopoly capitalism – are part of the problem.

The whole system has to go. The repressive police states have to be overthrown. The giant corporations have to be taken over. The super-rich have to be dispossessed. The old power structures have to be replaced with a new system of mass participatory democracy, of popular power from below, of ordinary people taking control of society and putting all our collective resources in the service of humanity.

The word for that is revolution. To save ourselves and our planet, we need nothing less than an international democratic revolution of the working class and the oppressed; that is, of the overwhelming majority of the people on the planet.

It is close to midnight. We have a decade or so to make the change. We have no time to lose. This book is a modest contribution to the task in hand. It is an appeal to get active, to join a revolutionary organisation, to become a maker of history not an object of history; an appeal not to remain sitting in the waiting room of the future, but to join the struggle to create a different future.

In the first part of the book, we analyse the many dimensions of the crisis, with chapters on the coronavirus pandemic, the accelerating climate disaster, the social collapse, the growth of slum cities, increasing police repression, the rise of fascism, and the economic roots of the crisis in chronic over-accumulation and debt-based financialisation.

In the second part, we discuss the strategy and tactics of resistance, with chapters on the limits of reformism, the limits of identity politics, and the need for mass united struggle from below by the working class and the oppressed on a global scale.

The great Italian revolutionary Antonio Gramsci, who died in a fascist prison, said of the crisis last time: 'The old world is dying, the new struggles to be born: this is a time of monsters.'

The new was smothered by Fascism and Stalinism in the 1930s. The consequence of this world-historic defeat for the working class and the oppressed was Stalingrad, Auschwitz, and Hiroshima.

This time, if we fail, it will be much worse. This time, we must win.

Chapter 1

Pandemic

How could this have happened? Someone propelled through a time warp from the 1960s would be astonished. Astonished to find a world laid low by a deadly virus. Astonished by economic collapse and mass unemployment. Astonished by looming environmental catastrophe. Astonished by an epidemic of police and military violence. Astonished that Europe allows thousands of migrants to drown in the Mediterranean. Astonished by a resurgence of the fascist politics of the 1930s. It would seem like they had landed in the middle of a dystopian science-fiction movie.

The capitalist world of the 1960s, and for a long time after, imagined it was making rapid progress towards ever greater prosperity, peace, democracy, freedom, and happiness – including, of course, the conquest of infectious disease. That self-image, promoted by conservatives, liberals, and social-democrats alike, was far from the whole truth, but it contained enough truth to convince many people, especially in the Western world, that they had 'never had it so good'.

In Western countries, living standards were improving for most people, and so was their health – particularly with wider use of antibiotics and vaccines, and with the provision of free or low-cost health services. Limited progress on these fronts was also made in some of the so-called 'Communist' countries, and even in some countries of the Global South – though many of the latter suffered appalling military devastation at the hands of imperialist powers.

Today, that ideology of progress based on liberal democracy, national development, and social welfare has collapsed. The self-confidence and optimism are gone. The world has become a dark place of corporate power, social collapse, and repressive violence.

We were warned. Since the 2008 banking crisis, repeated warnings have been issued, from across the political spectrum, that solving one financial meltdown by building another debt mountain could only result in another, yet more devastating economic collapse. Now it is upon us. The trigger last time was subprime mortgages. This time it is a deadly pathogen.

There had been countless predictions. From academic specialists, world health experts, leading public figures such as Barack Obama and Bill Gates, and not least from Marxist theorist Mike Davis in his bestselling 2005 book *The Monster at Our Door*. Davis warned that the appropriation of wild nature by capital, the industrialised rearing of animals in agribusiness complexes, the growth of mega-cities and their proximity to these complexes, and the desperate lack of basic health provision among the poor of the Global South were creating the conditions for a perfect storm of deadly viral infection on a world scale.

Few people, even on the Left, took Davis seriously. The relative ease with which the 2013-16 Ebola epidemic had been suppressed in West Africa – with 'just' 11,000 deaths – created a false sense of security. Ebola patients got sick within a couple of days of infection and often died rapidly. It was easy to see who was ill, and relatively easy to track those with whom they had been in contact.

Covid-19, by contrast, is a stealth virus. It causes mass infection, and transmission is easy and rapid. Yet the carriers are either asymptomatic or show symptoms only after a week or so of infection; the symptoms, moreover, vary widely in character and intensity, such that Covid often goes undetected even when it results in illness. This is ideal for spreading the disease unseen.

Deadly stealth is combined with potentially devastating immediate and long-terms effects on those seriously affected. The disease targets especially older people, those with weak immune systems or chronic respiratory problems (perhaps as many as 25% in the United States), and poor and ethnic-minority people. It is the biggest health challenge the world has faced since the so-called 'Spanish flu' of 1918-20. And it is one that neoliberal regimes in general, and far-right neoliberal regimes in particular – regimes harnessed to corporate power and the profit drive – are spectacularly incapable of meeting.

Who created the virus?

Where did the virus come from? Why did it spread so quickly? How have neoliberal governments responded? What is the relationship between the pandemic and the wider environmental, economic, and social crises of our time?

Much confusion surrounds the origin of the virus. This is partly because of deliberate political lying – like the rumour that it originated in a Chinese government laboratory in Wuhan. Also confusing is the fact that the causes of the pandemic are multiple. But everything is rooted in environmental and economic changes driven by the restructuring of agriculture, the creation of mega-cities, and global circuits of trade, transport, and travel – rooted, that is, in neoliberal capital accumulation.

The most insightful tracking of these intersecting factors has been the work of Mike Davis and also scientists Alex Liebman, Luis Fernando Chaves, and Rodrick Wallace, summarised in the American Marxist magazine *Monthly Review*. They argue that while some lethal pathogens stem from industrialised agriculture itself, most come from wild animals and spill over into human communities, either because of deforestation or because they are brought into the markets of major cities. They refer to 'the expanding peri-urban commodity circuits shipping these newly spilled-over pathogens in livestock and labour from the deepest hinterland to regional cities'.

Pathogens once contained in forest redoubts by their remoteness and the natural 'firebreaks' represented by biodiversity now find easy ways out – arriving in local markets as 'bushmeat' or following on the heels of livestock concentrations.

Transmission is facilitated by deforestation (for logging or to create vast monoculture complexes), which the authors refer to as the 'destruc-tion of environmental complexity which has previously kept pathogens in check'. Rapid export and re-export of agricultural commodities, as well globalised air travel, then completes capitalism's mechanism for produc-ing and spreading deadly diseases.

So the coronavirus that causes Covid-19 is not something new, but part of a pattern of pathogen transmission which has accelerated since the Millennium: 'The wide variety of pathogens, representing different taxa, source hosts, modes of transmission, clinical courses, and epidemiologi-cal outcomes, have all the hallmarks that send us running wild-eyed to our search engines upon each outbreak, and mark different parts and path-ways along the same kinds of circuits of land use and value accumulation.'

Creeping fascism and eugenic massacre

The precise origin of the virus – whether it came from a bat, a duck, or a monkey – is secondary. What really matters is the environmental, economic, and social framework that enabled its transmission. Central to its virulence has been the behaviour of far-right neoliberal regimes across the world.

The mainly right-wing and far-right governments that dominate the world today have transformed the pandemic into a massacre of the elderly, the sick, and the poor. Neoliberalism, with its laser focus on short-term business returns, has been unable to create strategies that simultaneously suppress the virus and sustain profits.

At the time of writing (October 2020), there have been about 45 million recorded infections and 1.2 million fatalities, according to the World Health Organisation (WTO). The WTO says the pandemic is out of control and getting worse in large areas of the world, especially the United States, Brazil, India, and much of Europe.

As Umair Haque explains, exploding virus transmission across the US is liable to make the disease permanent and risks the country becoming an isolated 'plague state':

> *At 100,000 cases a day or so, society begins to stop functioning almost entirely. Schools and universities stay shut. Banks and stores never open up. Hospitals and ICUs are overwhelmed. Just providing people the basics – daily water, food, energy, medicine – has now become a critical and crucial challenge. Society's basic systems of healthcare, education, finance, employment all begin to break, crash, and burn. Bang! There goes society.*

This may be overly pessimistic, but that it can even be discussed shows how perilous the situation has become, and how incompetent are the regimes responsible. It is striking that the governments with the worst record – the United States, Brazil, and the UK – are those with the most right-wing and cavalier pro-business regimes. All three governments were reluctant to go into lockdown and desperate to come out of it, so the pandemic was allowed to rage, increasing the death toll, the economic damage, and the long-term impact.

Among the countries most successful in suppressing the virus have been South Korea, Hong Kong, China, and Japan. They locked down early, created effective track-and-trace systems, and mobilised huge resources to provide protective clothing and other essential medical equipment. They were also the countries that enforced effective social distancing and quarantine measures such as sealing borders.

Brazil's central government was unwilling to do anything to counter the disease, which Bolsonaro described as 'a little flu'. Trump's government was less consistently philistine, but no national strategy emerged. In Britain, the Johnson government has had the ambition to 'flatten the curve' of the virus, but not suppress it – which would have involved a longer lockdown and comprehensive testing, tracking, and tracing.

The British government's initial flirtation with the quasi-fascist notion of 'herd immunity' – implying hundreds of thousands of deaths – revealed its central priority: staying open for business. Equally telling was its deliberate bypassing of medical experts, the NHS, local government, and community action, in order to hand lucrative contracts to private corporations for the provision of PPE, carrying out of tests, and the establishment of a track-and-trace system – with the entirely predictable consequence of serial failure.

The disease is not going away any time soon. It is now unlikely that it will ever be entirely eradicated, despite the vaccines. It could be much more effectively suppressed, but not so long as we are in the hands of neoliberal corporate regimes like the Bolsonaro, Trump, and Johnson governments.

In the medium term, the policies of these regimes are likely to prove economically catastrophic. The British economy has already gone off a cliff, with a 25% contraction in just two months (March and April 2020) and real levels of unemployment set to sky-rocket during 2021.

We are looking at economic damage on a scale not seen since the 1930s, and an economic collapse unprecedented in the history of capitalism.

Pandemic negligence

Neoliberal governments sabotaged pandemic preparation. The coronavirus puts in question the whole organisation of society. Governments are meant to plan and prepare for major crises, including health crises. In the US and Britain, they did the opposite.

In Britain, the post-2010 Tory government allowed stocks of protective equipment to degrade and go out-of-date, and suppressed the results of the 2016 NHS exercise (Operation Cygnus), which found that the health service was unprepared for a major pandemic.

This, of course, was because the government was ideologically hostile to the NHS. Prominent members of it had proclaimed their desire to see this public service sold off to private corporations. The NHS was consistently underfunded and allowed to run down. Bed occupancy in hospitals was between 94 and 98% before the pandemic – which meant they were effectively full-up. They were also chronically under-staffed, a problem made much worse by Brexit, with an estimated 40,000 European nurses either going home or never coming at all because of fears about residency status.

So the initial NHS chaos as the pandemic struck – lack of beds, lack of equipment, overworked staff, and, catastrophically, older patients infected with Covid being shunted back into care homes, where 30,000 have died of the disease – was due to a decade-long Tory programme of cuts.

The argument that health expenditure is being stretched by an ageing population is utterly bogus. The rich are getting richer, billions are wasted on arms, and there is always money for bank bailouts. The British government is currently creating hundreds of billions of pounds of new money to limit the economic damage of lockdown measures. Britain, in any case, spends less on health per capita than other leading European states.

In reality, the rundown of the NHS has been a 'softening-up' exercise, a preparation for widespread privatisation and the creation of a two-tier system where many procedures are only available privately. The disaster that would mean, especially for the poor and the elderly, can be observed in the United States, where people are sometimes forced to sell their homes to pay for essential medical care.

In Britain, the United States, and Brazil, government policy deserves to be called 'eugenic', because it involves the understanding – not openly admitted – that the old, the sick, and the poor would die disproportionately. Poorer working-class people tend to have more underlying health conditions, frequently poverty and stress related, and their jobs are often essential front-line jobs that cannot be done from home. This is the main reason that BAME people have been disproportionately hit by the virus.

In the UK, government eugenics is almost explicit. As long ago as 2013, the now Prime Minister Boris Johnson invoked pseudo-scientific notions of IQ to promote the idea that people 'who are already very far from equal in raw ability' might also be different in 'spiritual worth'. Toby Young, who worked for the Tory government in 2018, publicly advocated 'progressive eugenics' in 2015. The Tory MP Ben Bradley blogged that benefit claimants, described as a 'vast sea of unemployed wasters', should get vasectomies. One of Dominic Cumming's so-called 'super forecasters', Andrew Sabisky, has also promoted racist IQ claims and eugenics.

The most far-right neoliberal governments, including Britain's, have been responsible for tens of thousands of unnecessary deaths. But that is not just because Johnson, Trump, and Bolsonaro have made bad choices. They are managing a political system – neoliberal capitalism – which is experiencing simultaneous crises of economy, society, and environment, with morbid political consequences, notably the rise of far-right movements. Capitalism is increasingly incapable of upholding the life, liberty, and well-being of the overwhelming majority – those who are neither rich nor middle class.

Retreat from Camelot

When the 43-year old John F Kennedy was elected US President in November 1960, he seemed, with his brother, Attorney-General Robert Kennedy, to epitomise the spirit of post-war liberalism – capitalist certainly, but also democratic and socially progressive. Millions of people worldwide were taken in.

Kennedy came from a very rich family, organised the Bay of Pigs invasion of Cuba, initiated large-scale US intervention in Vietnam, and, with his brother, refused to prevent the Freedom Riders and other Civil Rights activists being murdered and brutalised in the American Deep South.

But the Kennedy entourage, especially the immediate family of the two brothers, including the conventionally glamorous Jackie Kennedy and brother-in-law film star Peter Lawford, were dubbed 'Camelot' after the court of the mythical King Arthur. For the increasingly affluent middle classes in the Western world, the Kennedys seemed to embody the spirit of the times.

After Kennedy's assassination in 1963, his successor Lyndon Johnson sent 500,000 troops to South Vietnam and started the genocidal bombing of North Vietnam. But he was also responsible for the 1965 Civil Rights

Act and the 'Great Society' project. Escalating imperialist war on the other side of the world did not preclude social reform at home.

The Great Society programme involved major government spending on welfare, medical care, transport, and both urban and rural poverty. The progressive spirit of the times was represented in Britain by the election in 1964 of Harold Wilson's Labour government with its promise of 'the white-hot heat of the technological revolution'.

Nearly 60 years on, the spirit of 'Camelot', and indeed the wider capitalist self-confidence of the boom years, has gone, buried beneath the devastation wrought by neoliberalism from 1979 onwards.

The turn away from the mixed-economy, welfare-state model that seemed to have worked so well between 1948 and 1973 was never a success. Growth rates in the neoliberal era were only ever half what they had been during the post-war boom. The economic system became highly dysfunctional – dominated by banks, debt, and speculation, with grotesque and ever rising levels of corporate power and social inequality. But even the neoliberal dystopia – with its competitive individualism, its greed and selfishness, its mindless consumerism and celebrity culture – is now falling apart.

Even if the coronavirus is suppressed – and there is no sign of that happening any time soon – the world economy will have taken its biggest hit since the 1930s, perhaps the biggest ever, and all the underlying problems will remain of a chronically unstable debt-based economy, worldwide social devastation, a serial breakdown of the international order, and a rapidly accelerating environmental crisis.

Chapter 2

Burning Planet

The Covid-19 pandemic is only one instance of an accelerating breakdown in the relationship between the human species and the natural world.

Humans are part of Nature. On the one hand, we are animals with material needs and organic form. On the other, our actions impact upon the rest of Nature, sometimes degrading it, sometimes remodelling it, always having an effect.

All the products of human labour are therefore part of Nature. Everything we do to provide ourselves with a livelihood involves drawing upon the resources of Nature and refashioning them into new forms.

These processes are not reversible, but they may be repeatable. If a glacier melts because the temperature rises, the water of which it is formed flows away. If a new glacier forms in the same place when the temperature falls again, it must be comprised of another body of water. In Nature, as in Society, everything is process and motion.

The energy involved in natural processes is a constant: it can be endlessly recycled, but it cannot be destroyed, so whatever you do, it will still be there in one form or another. This is one of the basic laws of physics (known as 'the First Law of Thermodynamics').

It follows that human beings may interact with Nature in ways that are 'renewable' or 'sustainable' – where energy is recycled in essentially repetitive ways – or in other ways that cause a metabolic 'rupture' or 'rift' – where energy is reconstituted as a destructive force.

Let us take two contrasting examples. A hoe-cultivator who harvests a garden plot of cassava, feeds the tubers and leaves to her pigs, and then lets them roam to manure the plot, is engaged in a recycling of energy that is ecologically sustainable.

Corporations that extract oil, refine it into petroleum, and then sell it to other corporations to burn in jet engines are doing something quite different: theirs is not a renewable process, but a release of carbon waste into the atmosphere and a permanent remodelling of the Earth's metabolism.

Previous human societies have experienced metabolic rifts. Pre-industrial societies often failed to keep the land 'in good heart', so that soil became exhausted or vegetation overgrazed. Sometimes entire civilisations were brought to collapse by human-made ecological disaster.

But there are critical differences between all pre-industrial societies and modern capitalism. The former were agricultural societies whose basic rhythms were determined by the cycle of the seasons; the latter is a system of competitive capital accumulation hard-wired by the profit motive for exponential growth. The former were always essentially local or regional, so that what happened in one place had limited impact in others; the latter is now a fully globalised system which has the whole of humanity and the entire global environment in its grasp.

Marx sensed this danger in his analysis of the system at its inception. He talked about the way in which the factory system and the growing separation between town and country were creating a rupture in the metabolic relationship between human beings and the rest of Nature.

William Morris, who was both a great artist and a revolutionary socialist, railed against environmental devastation and the way in which workers' lives were ruined by sweated factory labour, foul industrial cities, and lack of both leisure for self-development and access to the natural world.

Hugo Blanco, the Peruvian Marxist, peasant leader, and environmental campaigner, argues that the struggles of indigenous people in the Global South are inseparable from the defence of Nature against corporate power.

John Bellamy Foster, a leading US Marxist academic, has written a series of books analysing the links between Marxist theory, modern capitalism, and climate change. He has been in the forefront of the renewal of Marxist ecology in the face of the apocalyptic scale of the environmental disaster now unfolding.

Foster's contributions have been extended by those of other Marxist writers, from Geoff Mann and Joel Wainwright's book *Climate Leviathan*, which argues for an emancipatory movement of Marxist and indigenous struggles, to McKenzie Wark's ambitious *Molecular Red*.

Andreas Malm's *Fossil Capital* is also seminal. It attacks the conventional but deeply flawed historical view that traces the fossil economy to alleged scarcities. On the contrary, Malm argues, historical analysis shows that the transition to steam power was motivated by the fact that it allowed a greater subordination of labour to capital than the alternatives. This situates the climate crisis within the logic of capital accumulation itself.

It is impossible to exaggerate. The planet is slowly dying. It first became sick about 250 years ago, at the start of the Industrial Revolution, when the world economy began to grow at an exponential rate. The sickness is now approaching a terminal crisis.

The Covid-19 pandemic has, of course, triggered a global depression. The world economy was set to contract by about 5% during 2020. Further shocks – renewed lockdowns, disrupted supply-chains, a global financial crash, a succession of corporate bankruptcies – could deepen the depression in 2021. Falling demand and rising debt could mire the system in long-term stagnation.

But the world's political and corporate elites are determined to reopen for business (whatever the health risk), and their aim is a return to pre-pandemic 'normality' – that is, to the unplanned, unlimited, unsustainable capital accumulation that is destroying the planet.

Global production increased more than 80 times between 1750 and 1980. Nowadays it tends to double every 25 years. Because of this, energy consumption has soared. World coal production has risen from 15 million tons in 1800 to 8,000 million tons today. World oil production was 150 million barrels in 1900, but is now around 30 billion barrels a year.

Exponential economic growth has meant exponential growth in population and cities. The world was home to about 750 million people in 1750, 1.25 billion in 1850, and 2.5 billion in 1950; now it is 7.5 billion. Only 2.5% of a much smaller global population lived in cities in 1800. Today city-dwellers are the majority of humanity.

More output, more power, more people, more cities: the result has been massive strain on the Earth's resources. It takes many forms. Wild Nature is appropriated and deadly pathogens spread through agribusiness complexes and mega-city slums. Forests are cut down, wetlands drained, soils eroded. Water extraction turns farmland into desert. Habitats are destroyed and 75 species become extinct every day. Chemicals are dumped in oceans, lakes, and rivers. Toxins leak into groundwater. Fertilisers, herbicides, and pesticides contaminate food supplies. Landfills overflow with synthetic waste. Nuclear power plants melt down and fill air, land, and sea with carcinogenic particles. Plastic waste degrades into trillions of microscopic specks that infect every living organism.

But one dimension of the ecological crisis predominates. In the last 200 years, the burning of coal, oil, and gas has increased the amount of carbon dioxide in the atmosphere from 280ppm (parts per million) to 410ppm; and the rate of increase is accelerating.

The effects are already upon us. They take the form of storms and floods, droughts and bush-fires, with the rate of extreme weather events rising rapidly across the globe. In 2019, for example, Australian bush-fires destroyed an area the size of Britain, tropical cyclones did $60 billion of damage worldwide, and a total seven million people were displaced by climate impacts.

All the measures of climate change are on a steep upward curve. Some authorities predict that a further billion people will be plunged into extreme poverty over the next decade on current climate forecasts. Hundreds of millions will be displaced and forced to move as homelands are scorched into deserts.

The capitalist carbon machine
The international ruling class knows that we face climate catastrophe. They know that it threatens them and their system – not just the working class and the poor – and they would stop it if they could.

But they cannot. Their wealth and power are embedded in the world capitalist system and its relentless drive for expansion and profit.

We can easily measure the failure of the global political elite to manage the climate crisis by reference to the pitiful achievements of their flagship forum, the United Nations Climate Change Conference. This met for the first time in Berlin in 1995. Conferences have taken place every year since. They are attended by all the world's 193 nation-states.

For a quarter of a century, COP (Conference of the Parties) conferences have been the principal attempt to agree an international response to the global climate crisis. They have resulted in major 'agreements' like the Kyoto Protocol (1997) and the Paris Agreement (2015). It is now clear that these conferences have failed. This is evident in the following:

Accelerating carbon emissions
Only two billion tonnes in 1900, annual carbon emissions had reached 26 billion tonnes when COP met for the first time in 1995. They reached 34 billion tonnes in 2010, and hit an all-time high of 37 billion tonnes in 2018.

Accelerating atmospheric concentrations
Below 285ppm (parts per million) in pre-industrial times, atmospheric concentrations of carbon dioxide hit 330ppm in 1975, 350ppm in 1990, 375ppm in 2005, and now stand at 410ppm.

Accelerating temperature rises
Average global temperatures have risen by an estimated 1.2°C since pre-industrial times. Three-quarters of that warming has occurred since 1975. Half has occurred since 1995. The ten hottest years on record have all occurred since 2002. The year 2019 was the second hottest on record.

Accelerating polar-ice melt and sea-level rise
The average volume of Arctic sea-ice has roughly halved in the last 40 years. It is now declining at a rate of about 13% per decade. Comparable ice-melts are occurring in Antarctica and mountain regions like the Himalayas. For 2,000 years before 1900, global sea-levels were static.

Between 1900 and 1990, they rose by 1.2mm to 1.7mm on average. By 2016, the rate had risen to 3.4mm per year.

Accelerating climate-change impacts
More frequent and more intense heat-waves are causing increases in wild-fires, droughts, and desertification. Rising and warming seas are causing heavier rainfall, more serious flooding, more frequent mega-storms, and the inundation of coastal areas. These changes are driving the world's sixth mass extinction, with species loss running at 1,000 times the normal rate. Climate change is destroying livelihoods, increasing disease, and displacing people.

Accelerating risks of hitting one or more irreversible tipping-points
Changes in the Earth's ecosystem are characterised by both incremental shifts and sudden tipping-points. Among the tipping-points that may, sooner or later, be triggered by incremental global warming are: abrupt collapse of the West Antarctic ice-sheet; abrupt collapse of the East Antarctic ice-sheet; abrupt collapse of the Greenland ice-sheet; thawing of Arctic permafrost and release of methane gas; rapid deforestation of the Amazon; and failure of the Atlantic Gulf Stream. Some scientists fear a 'global cascade' of interacting tipping-points.

Whatever measure is chosen, the evidence shows that the global political elite have failed to halt climate change. It also shows that far more radical action is now necessary. It would be political idiocy – on the evidence of the last 25 years – to assume that the existing system will deliver what is necessary.

The failure of the global political elite is systemic. It is not that we do not know what to do. It is not that the wrong policies have been adopted. It is that the economic and geopolitical system – the current world order – cannot deliver the radical action necessary.

The OECD (Organisation for Economic Co-operation and Development), representing the world's leading industrial economies, considered the pre-pandemic global growth rate of 3% to have been too low. Yet a 3% annual growth rate means a doubling in the size of the world economy every quarter century.

The fossil-fuel corporations plan to extract twice the amount of coal, oil, and gas between now and 2030 than can be burned if we are to restrict global temperature rise to the 1.5°C 'aim' of the Paris Agreement.

This 'aim' is not ambitious enough: most climate scientists predict severe damage to the Earth's eco-system with this level of warming. But even this 'aim' falls well below the 'pledges' of the participants, which, even if implemented, are expected to result in a disastrous 3°C of global warming. Many leading scientists think we are heading for at least 4°C of global warming.

The ecological crisis has triggered global protests on a scale comparable with the anti-globalisation and anti-war protests of the early 2000s. Beginning in Britain in November 2018 and continuing around the world for the next year, tens of thousands of climate activists organised by Extinction Rebellion (XR) took part in a rolling series of direct-action protests, typically blocking roads and bridges, refusing to move, and allowing themselves to be arrested.

Overlapping with the XR protests, a succession of school climate strikes inspired by young Swedish activist Greta Thunberg took place during 2019; these involved a million people and 2,200 strikes in 125 countries on 15 March, and peaked at 4 million people and 4,500 strikes in 150 countries on 20 September.

The protests have pushed the ecological crisis right up the political agenda. Before the pandemic, one survey of opinion in eight major states showed a clear majority of voters in seven of those states citing it as 'the most important issue' – ahead of terrorism, migration, and the economy. Even in Britain – the exception – three-quarters agreed that climate change was driving extreme weather events, and two-thirds believed it was a direct threat to ordinary people and that 'time is running out to save the planet'.

Labour's Green New Deal was another measure of the political prominence of ecology. The 2019 Labour Conference agreed 'one of the most comprehensive ecological proposals ever put by a major political party challenging for office' (in Alan Thornett's words). It included a £400 billion 'National Transformation Fund' of which no less than £250 billion was to be funnelled through a 'Green Transformation Fund' dedicated to 'renewable and low-carbon energy and transport, biodiversity, and environmental restoration'. Labour was committed to creating a million climate jobs – on union rates and conditions – many of them in retrofitting all of Britain's 27 million homes for carbon efficiency.

The new Starmer leadership is already watering down Labour's Green New Deal. The Tories, of course, are travelling in the opposite direction. Though Tory Chancellor Rishi Sunak has promised £2 billion for the retrofitting of the housing stock, the amount is paltry against the scale of the problem, and must be set against the £25 billion earmarked for 'road improvement'. Post-pandemic, the carbon economy is to be rebooted.

There is a deeper problem – a systemic and existential problem for humanity and the planet. Even the most ambitious of green reformist policies – by which we mean policies compatible with, and therefore potentially achievable under, the dominance of capital – will be too little, too late to prevent disastrous ecological breakdown. That is the central lesson of 25 years of failure at COP.

The needs of humanity and the planet are represented by climate science, by declarations of intent from above, by the increasingly urgent demands of a growing mass movement from below, and by the programmes of some progressive political parties. But these needs – best met by a zero-growth, stable-state, carbon-neutral economy – are incompatible with the world capitalist system. Here is why.

Capitalism is the self-expansion of value
Growth – 'the self-expansion of value' – is inherent in the capitalist mode of production. It is expressed in Marx's formula M – C – M+, where M is the money originally invested, C is the plant, materials, and labour used in the production process, and M+ is the money originally invested recouped plus profit. This cycle endlessly repeats, making capitalism a dynamic system of perpetual growth. If the cycle fails – if there is no growth and therefore no profit – investment collapses and there is mass unemployment and mass impoverishment. Capitalism is incompatible with a zero-growth or stable-state economy.

The world is divided into warring states
Climate change is a global issue. It requires agreement and action on a global scale in the interests of the planet and humanity. But the world is divided into 193 separate nation-states, ranging from superpowers like the United States and China to countries of fewer than a million people like Luxembourg, Malta, and Tuvalu. Most of these countries invest heavily in armaments and engage in geopolitical competition with their rivals. The world's nation-states have killed at least 10 million people in their wars since 1945. They currently spend $1.8 trillion on armaments each year and have 21 million personnel in their armed forces. There are a dozen major wars currently raging. An estimated 70 million people are refugees from conflict. A world divided into warring states cannot be expected to make rational international decisions on climate.

The world is divided by grotesque class inequalities
The world's richest 26 people own the same amount of wealth as the poorest 50% of humanity. The six richest billionaires in Britain own the same amount of wealth as the poorest 13 million Britons. These inequalities have been growing since the 1980s, and the wealth gap between the global rich and the mass of the world's people is wider today than ever before in human history. Three billion people – nearly half the world population – live in poverty, and 1.3 billion live in extreme poverty. With a zero-growth or stable-state economy, satisfying the basic needs of the world's poor would depend upon redistribution of wealth – from the corporate rich to the international working class – on a historically unprecedented scale.

A wave of creeping fascism and climate nihilism
A wave of nationalism, racism, and fascism represented by authoritarian leaders and far-right parties is sweeping the world. The politics of the far

right is a combination of ultra-neoliberal corporate power and national-ist-racist reaction. Climate change is either denied or ignored. The Far Right represents climate nihilism.

Short-term systems and a long-term crisis
Capital accumulation involves circuits of capital in which investments are expected to deliver returns within a year, five years, at the most ten years. Each corporation has an essentially short-term perspective; one, moreover, that does not include such 'externalities' as environmental pollution. Political systems also operate on relatively short cycles, typi-cally those represented by the electoral calendar. Both capitalists and politicians are wedded to short-termism. The climate crisis, of course, is unfolding over decades.

This is the greatest crisis in human history. The survival of the existing plan-etary eco-systems and the socio-economic lifeways based upon them are at stake.

Because solutions must be a) zero growth, b) radically redistributive, and c) internationally determined and applied, climate catastrophe can be averted only by global revolutionary action to halt the carbon economy, take over the corporations, dispossess the rich, and create a new political order based on mass participatory democracy and popular control over natural resources and human wealth.

In the interwar period, socialists argued that the world faced a choice between revolution and barbarism. They were right. The Left was defeated, fascism triumphed, and the world experienced the barbarism of the Second World War and the Holocaust.

Today, the world faces a similar choice between revolution and extinc-tion. Either the Left builds a global mass movement for total system change – to create a new world based on democracy, equality, peace, and sustainability – or the capitalist system will destroy the planet.

Chapter 3

Social Crisis and Social Class

Three titans dominate global society: the corporations and the interna
tional capitalist class that controls them; the repressive state apparatuses
and the political and military elites that run them; and the vast mass of
humanity, the working class and the oppressed people of the world.

In this chapter, we focus on the third titan. We refer to the other two
– capital and the state – only in so far as they impact upon the third. But
that impact is huge, as the mass of the world's people, 85% of humanity,
are ground down by corporate power and state repression in a social crisis
of unprecedented dimensions.

But our third titan, the people, is not simply a victim, not simply a
great mass of the exploited and the oppressed: it is potentially the agent
of its own emancipation. For there is no other: the corporations and the
imperial-military-police states are embedded in a system hard-wired for
ecological catastrophe, permanent war, and social devastation. Only the
people have an interest in creating a new world based on democracy,
equality, peace, and sustainability. Only the people have an interest in
their own freedom.

The working class and the oppressed are both the victims of the
system and, potentially, its destroyers; they are both the objects of history
and, potentially, its subjects – the agents of revolutionary change, the
makers of a new history, an alternative future. Because of this, the start-
ing-point for all serious discussion of strategies for radical social change
has to be the nature of the modern working class.

This is a heavily contested matter. Neoliberalism and postmodernism have shrouded the question of class in ideological fog. Neoliberalism

has promoted the idea of individualism, aspiration, and 'being your own person', in the context of a 'free market' where anyone can 'get on' through their own efforts and talents, and where success is measured by income and material possessions.

Postmodernism – an influential academic theory that masquerades as progressive but is in fact deeply reactionary – reflects the dominant neoliberal ideology. Class and oppression, which are harsh material realities, are dissolved into multiple alternative 'identities', from which people can pick and choose, as if society were some gigantic cultural supermarket. Constructing 'difference' becomes an assertion of self. The splintering of society becomes 'empowerment'. The solidarity that is the very essence of mass struggle from below is systematically picked apart in the 'critical discourse' of the university seminar.

Here we defend the Marxist concepts of class and oppression, and we reassert the centrality of united mass struggle from below to any serious project of radical change. We start by returning to the immediate experience (at the time of writing) of the pandemic.

Class and Covid
The disease discriminates. It seeks out the weak, the marginal, the black and the brown. The virus replicates in migrant dorms and meat-packing factories, in shanties and *favelas*, in slum cities where people live stacked in concrete tenements. It spreads where whole families live in single rooms, the water is from standpipes, and public healthcare does not exist. It infects mainly the poor, and kills mainly the poor.

The plague is not an 'equaliser'. Even in the Global North, it discriminates, killing far more of the poor, the black, and the ailing than it does the rich and the middle class. The plague underscores the fracture lines of class inequality and racial oppression.

It does more than this: it exposes the negligence, incompetence, and corruption of neoliberal regimes aligned with corporate interests. It reveals that public health provision has been crippled by cuts and privatisation – crippled to the point of breakdown in a normal winter, crippled to the point of lethal danger in the context of pandemic.

And they were warned, again and again – warned that rampant agribusiness had become an incubator and transmitter of new viral diseases with pandemic potential, as the last domains of wild nature were penetrated, as ancient ecosystems were broken down and replaced with monocultures, as vast factory-farm complexes and new proletarian slums were constructed, and as global supply-chains were threaded across thousands of miles in a dozen directions.

The neoliberal regimes were warned. The experts knew the dangers. A succession of lethal outbreaks stretching back a quarter of a century had sounded the bell. But neoliberal governments did nothing, so when

Covid went global, there were not enough critical-care beds, or ventilators, or PPE, or test facilities.

Worse still, some remained in denial as the disease got a grip, still doing nothing, peddling fascist-eugenicist garbage about 'herd immunity' (initially the line of UK premier Boris Johnson and his shadowy advisor Dominic Cummings), or saying it was just 'a little flu' (Brazilian president Jair Bolsonaro), or claiming 'we have it totally under control' (Donald Trump). And when they did finally act, ever faithful to the corporate rich whom they serve, they funnelled government money to private contractors, working for profit, so the provision of PPE, of testing facilities, of track-and-trace procedures was bungled.

Thus did the disease expose much more than the fracture-lines of exploitation and oppression; it revealed a dystopian neoliberal order in which every official statement is a lie, every political act is spin, every public need is commodified and sold to profiteers.

The pandemic has revealed the evil essence of neoliberalism. It is not so much an economic doctrine – though the myths of 'free-market' capitalism provide the window-dressing – as an exercise in class warfare. Its very essence is an exponential increase in the gap between the world's richest and poorest.

The neoliberal counter-revolution

We can see the effects all around us. Take Britain. Following its test-run in Chile under the dictatorship imposed by the CIA-backed military coup in 1973, the neoliberal counter-revolution began with Britain's Thatcher government in 1979. The damage done to the social fabric in the 40 years since has been extreme.

All the indices of misery were rising sharply, even before the impact of the pandemic and the new depression: the suicide rate among disabled people whose benefits have been cut off; the number of rough sleepers who cannot afford a home; the proportion of families forced to access food banks; the number of children living in poverty; the growth of the gig economy with its low pay, long hours, and zero-hours contracts; the rising burden of debt carried by students, the poor, and ordinary working-class households.

Every conceivable statistical measure shows the trend, in each country, and in global perspective. The world's 2,150 billionaires have the same amount of wealth as the poorest 4.6 billion people who make up 60% of the global population. The 22 richest men in the world have more wealth that all of Africa's women. The top 1% control 50% of the world's wealth, the top 20% control 95%, the bottom 80% get by on just 5%.

Nothing like this has been seen in human history. The grotesque greed of today's lords of capital surpasses that of Egyptian pharaohs, Roman emperors, Renaissance princes, and even the Gilded Age robber barons of the late 19th century.

It has not arisen by accident, through the working of some 'hidden hand'; this is the voodoo economics of the system's apologists. It is the result of deliberate policy, of a class war waged by the few against the many over the last 40 years.

The quarter century following the Second World War was shaped by three main global trends: the nuclear-armed confrontation and global proxy wars of the two opposing superpowers ('the Cold War'); a long economic boom underpinned by state spending, especially arms spending, and US economic and financial pre-eminence; and a wave of anti-colonial 'national liberation struggles' in the so-called 'Third World'.

In the 'First World' – the Western capitalist democracies – a social-democratic or welfare consensus prevailed. Economic growth meant full employment, strong unions, and rising living standards. Governments were committed to Keynesian state intervention, redistributive taxation, and improved public services. Tory politicians claimed 'you've never had it so good'. Labour politicians talked of 'the white-hot heat of the technological revolution' and proclaimed a new era of 'mass abundance'. Academics spoke of the 'embourgeoisement' of the working class and conducted surveys of 'the affluent worker'.

In the 'Second World' – the Stalinist dictatorships of Eastern Europe – there was rapid state-managed industrialisation and marked improvement in living standards, housing, education, and healthcare. In the 'Third World' – the countries of the Global South emerging from colonial rule – newly independent regimes prioritised economic modernisation and social reform, winning a wide measure of popular consent for their 'national-developmental' programmes.

But the Great Boom slowed in the late 60s and finally came to an end with renewed crisis in 1973. This coincided with a global upsurge of mass struggle unlike anything seen since the 1930s. The system was so battered by both economic and political crisis between 1968 and 1975 that many believed revolution to be imminent.

But as the great social movements against oppression, war, exploitation, and dictatorship receded during the late 1970s, the international ruling class went onto the offensive. With slower growth, falling profits, and intensified competition, the system could no longer afford a 'social-democratic' consensus. The strong unions, high wages, social benefits, and public services built up during the Great Boom looked increasingly problematic. The radical demands of the mass movements of 1968 75 appeared utopian.

The neoliberal counter-revolution, pioneered in Britain under Thatcher and the United States under Reagan and then rolled out across the rest of the world, was an attempt to redistribute wealth from labour to capital by overturning the post-war consensus and reversing the advances made by working people since 1945. The rate of profit was to be restored.

Wealth was to be siphoned upwards to the rich, not downwards to the rest. A new era of unregulated 'get rich quick' capital accumulation was to be facilitated.

The re-engineering of the economy was contradictory and dysfunctional. Neoliberalism has exacerbated the system's long-term problems of over-accumulation (of capital) and under-consumption (by working people). We deal with this in Chapter 7. What concerns us here is the consequent remodelling of society, the growing chasm between rich and poor, and a global social crisis without precedent in human history.

The new working class

Capitalism is continuously transformative. Marx, writing at the infancy of the system, described this in a justly famous passage of *The Communist Manifesto* (1848):

> *The bourgeoisie cannot exist without constantly revolutionising the instruments of production, and thereby the relations of production, and with them the whole relations of society... Constant revolutionising of production, uninterrupted disturbance of all social conditions, everlasting uncertainty and agitation distinguish the bourgeois epoch from all earlier ones. All fixed, fast-frozen relations, with their train of ancient and venerable prejudices and opinions are swept away, all new-formed ones become antiquated before they can ossify. All that is solid melts into air ...*

So it has been – and continues to be – in the transition from the state-managed national capitalism of the post-war years to the neoliberal globalised capitalism of the last generation. Manufacturing has shifted from the Global North to the Global South. Finance, communications, and services have expanded massively. Old industrial centres have become 'rust-belt' zones of industrial and social collapse. Whole battalions of unionised labour have dissolved. Where once there were miners, dockers, ship-builders, and car-workers, now there are call-centres, warehouses, and superstores staffed by low-paid labour spied on by security cameras.

There is a new working class. It is black and white, women and men, migrant and indigenous. All of it is exploited – creating the wealth so much of which is then appropriated by the corporate rich – and many are also oppressed by racism, sexism, and homophobia.

We must define class, for there is much misunderstanding of this concept, and also much confusion about the relationship between exploitation and oppression.

Class has economic, social, and political dimensions. Economically, it revolves around the core process of exploitation, by which a minority ruling class extracts surplus from a majority working class. This happens in various ways.

Exploitation occurs in the workplace, where workers collectively produce wealth of greater value than the wages they are paid, with the difference taking the form of profit accumulated by corporate capital. The neoliberal counter-revolution was designed, in part, to increase profits by cutting wages, eroding conditions, and increasing workloads; and this was made possible by systematic union-busting to destroy collective organisation and atomise and precariatise the workforce.

Exploitation also occurs at the point of consumption and social repro-duction. Monopoly power means routine overcharging for goods and services. Interest payments on mortgages and other forms of debt flow into private banks. Extortionate rents enrich private landlords. The privatisa-tion of public services involves a recycling of tax revenues (paid by working people) into corporate profits. As ever more of society's collective wealth is 'commodified' – turned into something that can be bought and sold to make profit for capital – the social surplus increases at the expense of the working class.

Around this core process of surplus appropriation revolve various social relationships: a primary relationship between the ruling class (the inter-national bourgeoisie) and the working class (the international proletariat); and secondary relationships between sub-classes and sub-groups within classes, such as that between ('middle class') managers and ordinary work-ers in a workplace, or that between big corporations and small businesses.

The processes and relationships that constitute class are global. Nation-states and borders are historical constructs of capitalism. The working class is an international class with a collective interest in unity, struggle, and social transformation on a global scale. As Marx famously put it at the end of *The Communist Manifesto*: 'The workers have nothing to lose but their chains. They have a world to win. Workers of all countries, Unite!'

Marx was writing when capitalism was in its infancy and the proletar-iat – as opposed to the peasantry – but a tiny proportion of the working people of the world. Yet, even then, he saw capitalism as a global system and the proletariat as an international class.

It is far more so today. Indeed, in the neoliberal era, capitalism has become a totally globalised system, the first in human history, having penetrated into every pore of both society and Nature. This is a vital point. It is one of the reasons that the current crisis must be considered the greatest in human history. So let us pursue it a little further.

The colonisation of the planet

Capitalism is 'the self-expansion of value'. It grows exponentially, powered by the drive for profit, each round of accumulation immediately followed by the next on an enlarged scale. Over time, therefore, it eventually penetrates into, and percolates through, all the most distant recesses of the human and natural worlds – seeking resources to extract, labour to exploit, markets to dominate.

This process – evident to Marx, who wrote of it in the vivid terms quoted above – accelerates as the system expands, and the acceleration in the neoliberal era has been prodigious, driven in part by the system's chronic problems of over-accumulation and under-consumption. So virtually every part of the natural world, and the vast majority of the world's people, have now been subsumed into the process of world capital accumulation.

Modern capitalism is not only globalised to an unprecedented degree; it has also colonised more completely than ever before the planetary ecosystem and human society. Specifically, a rapid process of proletarianisation on a global scale over the last half century has largely destroyed the traditional peasantry, drawing vast masses into the global labour force, the majority of them condemned to remain 'precarious' or 'surplus'.

This means the contemporary crisis is more globalised than any previous crisis. There are no crisis-free zones in the modern world. All of the world's people are engulfed by the compound crisis of neoliberal capitalism – the pandemics of disease, the polluted Nature and climate turmoil, the chronic stagnation, the grotesque inequalities, the vast pools of surplus and displaced humanity, the growing arsenals of weaponry, the endless wars, the police repression, the racism and misogyny, and so much more.

So the global class structure becomes the lens through which we must analyse the social crisis. Amid the constant churn, where 'all that is solid melts into air', we can identify two great class forces – the ruling class and the working class – and an intermediate layer, the middle class, which plays a crucial and complex role in sustaining the social order.

The class structure of modern world capitalism

The world's labour force comprises approximately 3.5 billion of the world's 7.5 billion people. A tiny minority of about 1% constitutes the ruling class. These are the people who own and control the giant corporations and who run major public institutions. Their incomes represent shares in the distribution of social surplus. It makes no difference what form these shares take. There is no meaningful difference between 'fat cat' salaries to corporate directors, 'fat cat' dividends from share holdings, 'fat cat' speculation on the financial markets, and 'fat cat' corruption in state enterprise: all these are simply alternative arrangements for sharing out the spoils at the top of society.

Marx described the capitalist class as 'a band of warring brothers'. They compete for corporate advantage and personal advancement. They divide into factions with opposing interests – transnational capital versus national capital, banks versus industry, private corporations versus state enterprise, and so on. But the argument is strictly family. The capitalist class has a common interest in the exploitation of the working class and private appropriation of the social surplus; they stand united against any threat from below to their power and property.

The middle class makes up about 15% of the world's population. It comprises two main groups: the owners of medium-size businesses; and relatively secure, comfortable, well-paid managers and professionals, some working freelance, some formally employed, many of whom are involved in supervising and policing the labour of the working class. The middle class, long established in the Global North, is now fast-growing in the Global South. Because of its position, it tends to identify with the ruling class and share its world outlook: it is the natural mass base for all forms of right-wing politics.

The working class – and residual communities of peasant farmers – make up the remaining 85% of the world's population. We define the working class not as sociologists do, but as socialists must, if we are to make proper sense of the world; that is, we define it in terms of the core process of exploitation. The working class includes all those who live by their own labour, who are paid less than the value of their labour, who are, therefore, excluded from any share in the distribution of the social surplus. This includes many small-business owners, self-employed people, freelancers, workers in the gig economy, and so on. It certainly includes many 'professional' workers – teachers, health workers, civil servants, local government officers, etc – often classified as 'middle class'. And it has to include huge numbers of marginalised people who would work if they could, but who are denied the opportunity.

The global working class comprises three broad categories: a core working class of people who have a measure of job security, better pay and conditions, and usually a level of education or skill that gives their labour higher value on the jobs market; a precarious working class of people employed on short-term contracts, perhaps part-time or 'zero hours', with lower pay and worse conditions; and a marginal working class or 'reserve army of labour' – people largely surplus to the requirements of the system – who are only occasionally employed or not employed at all, and who are dependent on benefits or eke out a living in the informal sector.

The former group is relatively larger in the Global North, the latter two in the Global South; but all groups are represented across the world economy. Thus, whereas one in five (7 million) workers in Britain are precarious (or marginal), the global proportion is more than 60%. Migrant workers account for a huge proportion of the precarious and the marginal. One in three of the world's workers today – 1 billion people – is a migrant, 750 million internal to their country of origin, 250 million working abroad.

Neoliberalism has meant not just growing inequality and rising poverty; it has also involved mass displacement, an epidemic of insecurity, lives turned upside down, and families and communities torn apart.

This is the meaning of class: this lived human experience of exploitation and oppression; this social misery visited upon the many by the few in the interests of profit.

It is economic and social *processes* rooted in capital accumulation that give rise to class. This means that class itself is a *process* – it is endlessly reproduced, and, as the system evolves, endlessly reconfigured. So there is a class 'structure', but not in the sense of a rigid set of closed categories, like a caste system, only in the sense in which a growing plant may be said to have structure; in other words, class is an organic phenomenon in an eternal state of flux.

The process of class formation (and re-formation) happens regardless of whether people are aware of it. Indeed, the reality of it is veiled behind a thick smokescreen of right-wing ideology, pumped out constantly through all forms of media, the effect of which is to bamboozle people about their true condition and interests. The essence of socialist politics, in a sense, is that it seeks to disperse the fog and reveal the ugly reality of class society.

This brings us to the third aspect of class: class as a political force. When working people become aware of their true condition, and when they begin to organise to protect and advance their true interests, they become a political force and a potential agent of radical change. The aim of socialist politics is to change what is sometimes called 'class in itself' (the mere economic and social existence of class) into 'class for itself' (working people organised, mobilised, and fighting back).

We return to this – the working class as political force and agent of radical change – in the second part of this book. Before that, however, we want to deepen our understanding of the multi-dimensional character of the world capitalist crisis.

Chapter 4

Mega-Slums

The majority of the world's mega-cities – with 10 million or more inhabitants – are in the Global South. The majority of the people who live in them are poor. These mega-cities are also mega-slums.

This is a time of huge flows of people within and between countries, as the desperate rural poor and refugees from violence and climate catastrophe seek somewhere to establish a viable life. Global capital attempts to police this mass of people, to draw it into insecure labour when profitable, then spit it out as 'surplus humanity' when no longer useful.

We are around two decades along from when the majority of humanity lived in the countryside and worked in agriculture. The mega-slums of the Global South have been created in large part by the predatory expansion of agribusiness at the expense of peasant farms.

The cities in wealthier Western countries are themselves sites of increasing poverty and inequality. Forty years of neoliberalism and more than a decade of austerity have made labour for millions more precarious and less well-paid. Social welfare nets have been shredded. This has been made especially obvious during the Covid crisis. Take just one example: in New York, poorer, mainly Black and Hispanic, areas were hardest hit.

For many, though, especially the wealthy and affluent, cities are magical – centres of culture, the focus of employment, the places where the restaurants, bars, and clubs of an exciting social life can be found. Nothing could be further from reality for most of the hundreds of millions who live in the mega-cities of the Global South. As they grow bigger, they become centres of unimaginable human misery – a tragedy of unemployment, inequality, slum housing, random violence, and endemic ill-health. This is where 'the wretched of the earth' are especially concentrated.

Although under-reported, and with few reliable statistics, the world's mega-cities have become raging centres of the Covid pandemic. From Sao Paulo to Karachi to Lagos, these centres of poverty and packed insanitary housing have become natural breeding-grounds of the virus. The effects have spread out into the urbanised corridors around the mega-cities.

But the sources of this mountain of misery are often misunderstood. Naturalist David Attenborough is the most prominent of those who claim there are just 'too many people'. But that is not why the mega-cities grew, or why so many of them face such an appalling social crisis. The basic causes are the imposition of agribusiness in the countryside, and the destruction of state services and public employment by IMF-imposed 'restructuring' in the 1980s and 1990s.

Neoliberal globalisation has effectively destroyed nationalist governments and national-developmental programmes aimed at some sort of improvement for the masses, through, for example, state employment, infrastructure investment, and public health provision. All this was wrecked by IMF and World Bank 'conditionalities' attached to major government loans.

Neoliberalism has created legions of people who are literally 'surplus humanity', either unemployed, working in the informal economy, or forced to migrate, often ending up as 'illegal' people in economically more advanced countries. William I Robinson and Yousef K Baker see this 'surplus humanity' as a modern-day version of the Victorian 'lumpen-proletariat' ('lumpen-precariat' in their terminology), an intermittently employed 'reserve army of labour', used to push down global wages – either as cheap workers in the Global South or immigrant workers in developed countries. Police control of the migrant flows generated by this 'surplus humanity' is a crucial task of the emerging 'Global Police State'.

The mega-cities are not natural phenomena. The hundreds of millions of peasants and rural workers who make the decision to up sticks and relocate to them – many harbouring impossible dreams of middle-class lifestyles – are impelled by poverty to do so. Life in the mega-cities – even in the awful slums of places like Mumbai – can offer more opportunities to make a living than in subsistence-based rural villages.

Mexico City is a classic example of why mega-cities grow. Every day thousands of newcomers arrive from the countryside and build new *barrio* districts or join existing ones, to add to the already huge population of 23 million (more than Portugal and Belgium combined). For the most part, the new arrivals are victims of modern Mexico's version of what Marx called 'primitive accumulation': neoliberal 'reform' of landownership – that is, handing the countryside over to agribusiness corporations – under Carlos Salinas de Gortari, president from 1988 to 1994.

The Salinas 'reforms' ended the *ejido* system of collective land ownership by peasant farmers and cleared the way for the sale of peasant plots in line with the NAFTA free-trade agreement with the US and Canada. NAFTA also opened the Mexican market to huge imports of American food, further hitting the peasant producers of Mexico's villages. Peasants formerly engaged in collective farming either became impoverished (mainly seasonal) farm labourers, or, more often, were pushed out completely by the new system. Trekking to the cities became an escape from hunger. Far better to scratch a living as an *ambulante* street-pedlar in Mexico City than to starve in the countryside.

The consequences of this immense concentration of humanity – 23 million in a space much smaller than Greater London – are deadly for the environment and the health of local people.

The new *barrios*, where arrivals are often harassed and robbed by the police, do not at first have basic amenities like sanitation. So people dig their own trenches, and what the sun dries out is often blown into the atmosphere – already polluted by cars and factories. A survey in the late 1990s showed that all of the city's thousands of street-food stalls had offerings infected with faecal matter.

Employment crisis

The poor in the mega-cities face linked crises of employment, housing, security, education, and health that make their lives next to impossible. Stable employment and decent wages are fundamental, but for hundreds of millions of the world's people today they are not available.

Many of the urban poor in and around mega-cities are pulled into the global production networks of neoliberal capitalism. These are the urban poor who work in the garment sweatshops of Bangladesh, the huge electronics factories in China, the garment and footwear factories of Indonesia and Vietnam, and the assembly plants of the *maquiladora* belt along the Mexico-US border. These workers often endure long hours for low pay in bad working conditions. In many places they are young women, regarded as more pliable, and having good eyesight and dexterity for work in the garment and electronics business.

Even if there is little or no job security, they are the lucky ones. In this semi-formalised sector, there is the possibility of long-term employment and some minimal economic security. But for most of the mega-city poor, who have to work in the unregulated informal sector, the situation is bleaker.

Classic jobs in the informal sector are things like a pedicab driver, a street pedlar (selling almost anything), a worker on a food stall, or someone forced into criminal activity like drug dealing or prostitution. As Paul Martin reports:

> *As there are limited positions available in the formal economy, many urban dwellers resort to working in the informal sector, which plays an important role in mega-cities. The informal economy comprises half to three-quarters of all non-agricultural employment in developing countries, and includes those parts of a country's economy that lie outside any formal regulatory environment. The informal sector accounts for 65% of all jobs in Dhaka, approximately 50% of Mexico City's workforce, and 25-30% of Bangkok's urban population... Jobs in the informal sector are often low in pay, labour intensive, low in productivity and security, have poor working conditions, and have great potential for exploitation, especially of children.*

The employment crisis fuels the huge waves of emigration from the Global South – of desperate people in search of a better life, or indeed any sort of life.

Wealth, corruption, and squalor

Former Labour cabinet minister Peter Mandelson notoriously said that he was extremely comfortable with some people being filthy rich. He forgot to add that some people are filthy rich because many millions are dirt poor.

In the Global South this is true everywhere; in the worst cases nearly all the wealth is captured by a small elite and the Western companies they collaborate with, and their dominance is enforced by police violence, electoral fraud, and corruption. This rebounds into the crisis of the mega-cities. Take Lagos, the major metropolis and former capital of Nigeria.

Nigeria is Africa's richest country, yet, among its 195 million people, 130 million lack adequate sanitation, 57 million lack safe water, 10 million of its children get no schooling, and between 12 and 22% of its youth are jobless. Mass urban and rural poverty have led to a semi-collapse of state functioning, while a corrupt officer caste are incapable of fighting the reactionary Islamic insurgency of Boko Haram in the north.

The dominant foreign currency earner is oil, but its revenues are stolen by the tiny elite who control the army, the political parties, and the government. The specific form of economic theft by the capitalist elite is corruption, which is all-pervasive. How does the corruption-theft system work?

The Nigerian example is just an extreme version of how numerous neoliberal elites in the countries of the Global South operate. At the top, all the major party groups have been captured by kleptocratic capitalists. Elections are about who is going to rob the state and the people. Corruption cascades from above into every sector of economic and public life. Crucial is the 'brown envelope' corruption aimed at keeping journalists and the media onside. Key economic sectors like the oil industry divide up the spoils with government ministers; the army and police are also key recipients of huge fortunes.

A grotesque example from elsewhere in Africa is the case of Isabel dos Santos, daughter of the former Angolan President Eduardo dos Santos. Isabel dos Santos had herself made head of the Angolan state oil company, Sonangol, and then stole the money – all of it, or at least many years' worth of oil profits. In one transaction she paid $57 million from the oil company to a friend for unexplained 'consultancy services'. At one point the state oil company was left with just $309 dollars in its account. Western finance and accountancy companies like Britain's Price Waterhouse Cooper were deeply involved in the management of de Santos' international financial operations.

In January 2020 she was charged with corruption in Angola, but is believed, at the time of writing, to be still at large somewhere in Europe. The Angolan government is demanding the return of $2 billion in all. The moral of the story is that if you control large parts of a state's financial resources, you have to spend it around, not keep it all for yourself, or the rest of the equally corrupt capitalist elite will turn on you.

The Nigerian ruling class is more careful than dos Santos to share the spoils; but the pillage of the people is no less. Instead of using oil wealth to boost the collapsed infrastructure of Lagos, the rich are trying to seize pitiful waterfront slums to build luxury housing. In April 2017 Remi Adekoya reported:

> This month, thousands of Nigerians have been rendered homeless after police stormed Otodo-Gbame, a riverbank community in the country's commercial capital, Lagos, razing homes and chasing away residents with bullets and teargas. This comes after 4,700 people in the settlement had their homes demolished in March, and 30,000 were evicted last November, so altogether tens of thousands of people have been systematically chased off lands that they have inhabited, in many cases, since the colonial era.

Adekoya accurately pinpoints the relationship between state power and wealth in Nigeria – and hundreds of cities worldwide:

> On paper, all Nigerians have rights. In practice, state power is often brazenly deployed to subjugate the poorest and weakest citizens in the interests of the rich and powerful, who usually operate above the law. Hence, Nigerians often say the only true crime in Nigeria is being poor. In a state where to be poor means to be utterly powerless and stripped of dignity, many see wealth as the only means of safeguarding themselves from such wanton oppression, a perception which helps propagate the corruption Nigeria has become notorious for, as many resolve to get rich by any means necessary.

According to Leilani Farha, the United Nations Special Rapporteur on housing, Lagos has some of the worst housing in the world. 'People are living in some of the worst, if not the worst, conditions I've seen in the world,' she says, 'and I've been to all the big slums in India, Kenya, South Africa.'

But Lagos is in the middle of a construction boom. Huge apartment towers are going up, intended to house wealthy Nigerians and foreign oil-workers. The occupants of the slums, on the other hand, face multi-dimension poverty – of income, housing, health, education, and security. The poor are the victims of every conceivable type of crime. Murder, robbery, sexual violence, and the kidnapping and trafficking of young women are rampant. But the police in the mega-cities of the Global South are not there to defend the people. This epidemic of lawlessness is especially prevalent in the Brazilian *favelas* and the South African townships, which are among the murder capitals of the world.

Gangs, drugs, and femicides

The counterpoint to the rambling slums of the Global South are the gated communities and flashy shopping malls of the rich and affluent. Often, as in Rio de Janeiro, the gated communities are cheek-by-jowl with the townships and slums, but the latter are no-go areas for anyone but residents, because of the level of crime; in Brazil, they are more-or-less completely controlled by drugs-based criminal gangs.

To be poor in the mega-cities is often to be faced with extreme danger – from both the police and violent criminals. This is especially true for women. In places which are desperately poor and where police rarely go – like the South African townships – sexual violence and rape are routine. Where the police and criminal gangs are actively engaged in the perpetration of sexual violence, the situation is particularly grim.

The Mexican city of Ciudad Juárez on the US border has become a world centre for the mass murder of women – femicide. María Encarnación López says that between 2010 and 2018 more than 900 women were reported murdered, and that since the mid-1990s more than 30,000 in total have disappeared. Mexico's National Femicide Reporting Observatory says that an average of six women a day are murdered in Ciudad Juárez. Most victims are found strangled, stabbed, dismembered, and torched in sewers, rubbish dumps, vacant lots, and river beds around the city. Nearly all the victims are young women workers, often single mothers and family breadwinners, who have jobs in the *maquiladora* factories which manufacture or assemble goods for export to the US.

Nearly all these crimes are unsolved, most never investigated, and human rights organisations believe the police are involved. Most of the murdered women – because they tend to be young, single, visible, and independent – are objects of resentment and are seen as 'soft targets' in a highly misogynist society. The Mexican authorities are inclined to avoid demands for an investigation into their deaths by labelling them as 'prostitutes' – as if that somehow makes their deaths justifiable. The *maquiladora* system, complicit police, and an intensely patriarchal culture combine to prevent effective action against the pandemic of femicide – despite mass protest both in Mexico and internationally.

Environmental crisis

The Global South's mega-cities are giant centres of environmental destruction. Take, again, the example of Mexico City. Because of the vast demand for water, the aquifer under the city is drying out. Like Indonesian capital Jakarta – an even bigger mega-city – Mexico City is sinking. Eventually it will become uninhabitable because of lack of drinking water and building collapse. Mexico already has one of the highest rates of water-borne gastroenteritis in the world. More affluent people get their water delivered in giant plastic bottles. Waste water ('black water') eventually finds its way to the surrounding countryside, polluting agricultural land in addition to the city. Fruit and vegetables have to be disinfected before consumption.

The city's air pollution is notorious, a product of cars, buses, and lorries, as well as the factories around the city edges. The five million cars registered in Mexico City jam the urban motorways, while the majority of people travel on the ultra-cheap metro and buses, or, if they can afford it, the huge number of taxis.

Air pollution and water contamination combine with packed housing to make ill-health 'normal' for the city's poor. And, of course, Mexico City is a major contributor to the greenhouse gases that cause global heating.

Each of the Global South's mega-cities has these, and other, environment problems in different combinations. Kinshasa, capital of the Congo, has no city-wide waste disposal system. Rubbish fills the streets. When flooding comes, the situation becomes intolerable as massively contaminated water fills the houses of the poor – a typical problem in the mega-cities.

There is no way out of the escalating environmental crisis of the world's mega-cities short of a massive redistribution of wealth in favour of the poor and public infrastructure. But this is not profitable – not to the police and gangsters who control the slums, not to corrupt local elites, not to the giant corporations that profit from the human and ecological devastation across the Global South.

Covid-19 in the mega-cities

Nobody knows how many people in Lagos have the virus, but if it is not widespread now, it soon will be. For the moment, the Nigerian epicentre of the virus is the northern city of Kano, the country's second city, with a population around four million. The gravediggers there say they are working overtime. And so many doctors and nurses have been infected that few hospitals are accepting new patients.

Kano's state government, until recently, claimed that a spate of unusual deaths was caused not by the coronavirus but by hypertension, diabetes, meningitis, or acute malaria. There is little social distancing, and few people are being tested. But doctors in Kano say that the disease is rampant and thousands have died.

Covid-19 has crashed into the Latin American mega-cities and their surrounding urban corridors because their physical and social structure makes their occupants particularly vulnerable. A crystal-clear example is the rampage of the pandemic through the *maquiladora* towns and cities on the Mexican side of the US-Mexico border. This corridor runs from Tijuana (twin city of San Diego) in the west, to Ciudad Juárez (twin city of El Paso), to Matamoros on the east coast.

Hundreds of low-paid *maquiladora* workers have died and thousands have been become sick. At least 400 workers in Baja California's *maquiladora* industry have tested positive, and at least 83 factory employees have died. Baja California is adjacent to San Diego County in the US, where infections and deaths are 25 times lower. A good number of the deaths on the Mexican side of the border are among younger people – people under 50, many in their 20s and 30s.

What explains this epidemic and the deaths among younger people? According to Mexican health experts, there are two key factors. First, many locked-down *maquiladora* companies came under pressure from US companies to re-open to supply US car plants, suffering from a lack of parts. Second, though the workers in the *maquiladora* companies are overwhelmingly young, they often lead highly stressed lives and occupy cramped, overcrowded housing.

None of the *maquiladora* cities is a mega-city, but the corridor as a whole is the equivalent of one and reproduces the patterns of employment that you find in many cities of the Global South – part of the workforce drawn into low-paid work for capital, another part focused on the informal sector. According to Nina Ebner and Mateo Crossa,

> The Mexican government, and the association of maquiladora companies, are opening centres on the Mexican border to receive 'illegal' immigrants sent back from the US. From there they will be pressurised to seek employment in the maquiladora factories and workshops. Many of these workers come from Central America, not from Mexico…
>
> We are witnessing a joint effort between the US and Mexican governments to deepen labour precarity along the border… anti-migrant policies and the militarisation of the US-Mexico border are integral to maintaining a low-wage labour force in northern Mexican border cities… the low wages of maquiladora assembly-line workers have long been key to the competitiveness of Ciudad Juárez in a restructuring global economy.

The virus has been through other parts of Latin America, hitting Ecuador and Brazil particularly hard, with Peru not far behind. At first the Ecuadorian city of Guayaquil was the hardest hit, but now Brazilian cities have caught up, especially the mega-city and economic centre Sao Paulo – one of the most unequal cities in the world.

Far-right Brazilian president Jair Bolsonaro refused to contemplate a lockdown because 'the spread of the virus is inevitable'. So far (at the time of writing) there have been 40,000 deaths in Sao Paulo state, most of them in the city. But the virus affects different social classes in different ways. Despite Bolsonaro, the swanky bars and restaurants in affluent areas are all closed down. So are the gleaming high-rise towers of the financial district. But the impoverished millions in the *favelas* cannot stay at home. Dejair Batista, a hairdresser in Brasilandia, one of the biggest *favelas*, told CNN reporter Daniel Motta, 'If you stay at home, you'll just starve to death.'

Brasilandia is the deadliest neighbourhood for Covid-19 in the city, with hundreds of deaths. Many local people work in the informal economy, which has all but disappeared during the virus outbreak, and now have to queue for food handouts. As in all *favelas*, social isolation is very difficult. Multiple generations are often packed under one roof, and there are few public parks or other outdoor spaces. For healthcare, there are clinics, but no big hospitals. And for the people in the locality who can afford to buy food, it means visiting local markets, which are virus hotspots in many Latin American countries. The whole of Brazil is short of doctors and nurses, and the universal healthcare system created in 1988 is 'universal' in name only.

According to the city's Health Secretary Edson Aparecido, the virus was brought back from Colorado ski resorts like Aspen, and then spread outwards to the poorer *favelas*, where the impact has been much greater than in middle-class areas. In mid-May the city's healthcare system was said to be near collapse. Of course, the affluent go private and their healthcare is not in danger. Brasilandia is a classic case of poverty creating or magnifying ill-health.

Rebel mega-cities

Workers and the poor have been crucial to some of the most important radical movements worldwide in the last 20 years. But the situation varies markedly from city to city and country to country, because the structure of employment and local political traditions are different. In the Bangladeshi capital Dhaka, for example, hundreds of thousands are concentrated in sweatshops supplying the global garment trade, and trade unionism is strong.

The *barrios* and *favelas* in countries like Brazil, Venezuela, and Bolivia have been crucial sites of support for the left-wing governments that came to power in Latin America from 1999 onwards. The explosion of support for the Workers Party in Brazil, the 'Chavist' movement in Venezuela, and Evo Morales' Movement Towards Socialism (MAS) in Bolivia represented a spontaneous understanding of something fundamental: that the struggle in the cities poses problems that cannot be resolved at city-level. A glance at the so-called 'water wars' in the Bolivian city of Cochabamba in 2000 makes this clear.

In 1999, at the 'suggestion' of the World Bank, the Bolivian government proposed Law 2029 to privatise Cochabamba's water supply and sell it to a new company, Aguas del Tunari, a consortium of local and international capital, including Bechtel of the US (massive profiteers during the Iraq occupation) and Abengoa of Spain.

This was an almost pristine-pure example of David Harvey's description of neoliberalism as 'accumulation by dispossession'. Prior to the privatisation, 80% of the one million people in the greater Cochabamba area had their water supplied very cheaply. Afterwards, under the new law, they were not even allowed to collect rainwater, which henceforth was the 'property' of Aguas del Tunari. Water bills shot up.

The result was months of near insurrection, with workers and local peasants taking over the city, thanks to the forging of an alliance between factory workers and local community and peasant organisations. Faced with this, the government eventually backed down.

One of the movement leaders, Oscar Olivares, recounts in his book ¡Cochabamba! how a poor middle-aged woman came up to him when they discovered they had won and said, 'Okay, so we won on the water supply, but what have we really won? My husband struggles to find work, I have to sell things in the street, and I cannot afford to educate my kids.'

So there was a sequel. The government defeat in the water wars started a near-insurrectionary movement that eventually brought down two corrupt presidents and led to the election of left-wing president Evo Morales in 2006.

The woman who spoke to Oscar Olivares had put her finger on a crucial point. There are mega-city battles over land and resources all the time, often involving the attempt to dispossess slum dwellers and the poor of their land and all-too-meagre resources. But where do these battles end up? What is really needed is a unified movement for radical social change across the issues and campaigns; one that can fuse into a movement for popular power at a national level.

Everywhere, radical movements face ferocious resistance from the rich, backed by international capital. Remi Adekoya's insights on Lagos apply across the Global South. In countries where the real crime is to be poor, the rich know they cannot afford to give an inch. You stay rich or you descend into hell. To remain on top they will resort to any amount of corruption, crime, and violence. In any case, relatively secure inside their gated suburbs, they subcontract the business of social control to the army, the police, and, if necessary, armed thugs. Their contempt for the poor – 'the wretched of the earth' – is visceral and vindictive.

But the enemy of the urban masses of the Global South is not just venal local elites, but transnational capital as a whole. Transnational corporations are hand-in-glove with local elites in stealing the oil of Nigeria, Ghana, and Angola, exploiting the labour of garment workers in Bangladesh, Vietnam, and Indonesia, and in appropriating the mineral wealth of the Congo and South Africa.

The internationalisation of capital should give rise to international solidarity with the struggles of the peoples of the Global South – the struggle against the land-grabs of the rich, the struggle for democracy, and the fight against IMF-World Bank privatisation and 'restructuring'. In the era of transnational capital, the fate of 'surplus humanity' is linked to the fate of workers and the poor everywhere.

Chapter 5

Police States and Warfare States

On 1 June 2020, to clear a space near the White House for a Trump photo opportunity, peaceful demonstrators were attacked by a combination of Park Police and Secret Service agents. The attack was unlawful, half an hour before the curfew kicked in. Police used tear-gas grenades, rubber bullets, shields, and batons, causing numerous injuries. Journalists were assailed too, including a TV crew from Australia, provoking protests from their government.

This was just one moment in a nation-wide US police offensive against demonstrators at a level of ultra-violence not seen since the attacks on Civil Rights demonstrators in the 1960s.

The violence that shocked the media in June 2020 was very visible: the whole world was watching because Trump had summoned the cameras. The violence meted out to Black Americans on a daily basis is not so visible – and it was the fact that the murder of George Floyd was captured on video that for a brief moment pulled back the curtain and triggered a global mass movement against violent police racism.

The uprising following the murder of George Floyd was prefigured by the August 2014 revolt in Ferguson, a Black suburb of St Louis, when an unarmed Black teenager, Michael Brown, was shot dead by a white police-man. Protests and riots erupted. Millions worldwide then watched news bulletins with incredulity as the Ferguson Police Department went into action wearing military-style uniforms, using an armoured car, carrying an arsenal of lethal weapons, attempting to enforce a curfew and disperse the crowds.

American social theorist William I Robinson has coined the term 'Global Police State' to describe the worldwide increase in police and military repression against radical and progressive opponents of neoliberal exploitation and oppression.

He does not mean that there is a single worldwide state with a unified Gestapo-like repressive force. He is talking about the massive increase in the use of police power to maintain right-wing rule, and the growth in the size and reach of a series of interlocking national security/police institutions, which increasingly co-ordinate data-gathering and operations across national boundaries.

Characteristics of the Global Police State include:

- The attempt to make the 'overhead costs' of radical and democratic protest much higher, through the use of police-military violence, mass arrests, and imprisonment.
- The attempt to designate oppositionists as 'terrorists'. Trump announced that he would designate 'Antifa' – Anti-Fascist Action – a terrorist organisation. In fact, Antifa was a tiny component of the Black Lives Matter anti-racist uprising, and the threat to label them as terrorists was a cynical device to de-legitimise the mass protests. Real terrorists, like the Ku Klux Klan and other far-right groups, have Trump's sympathy and support.
- The use of new types of weapons, or more lethal types of older weapons, that cause more grievous injuries.
- Introducing new laws severely restricting the right to publish critical material, the right to protest through demonstrations, pickets, and occupations, the right to belong to trade unions, and the right to organise opposition political parties.
- Attacks on critical media. Trump repeatedly attacked what he called 'fake news' – by which he usually meant mainstream liberal newspapers and TV channels. In the recent BLM uprising, police attacks on journalists were deliberate and widespread. In Minneapolis, photo-journalist Linda Tirado was blinded in one eye by a rubber bullet. Trump afterwards widened the attack to include platforms like Facebook and Twitter, hinting that he would look at laws to restrict the kind of political material they could carry. This was a very serious threat to democratic rights.
- The use of new methods of online data harvesting and surveillance to create what Michel Foucault called a 'Panopticon' state. The Panopticon was a prison designed by British philosopher Jeremy Bentham, where the guards from a central point could see into every cell, so that every prisoner was potentially under surveillance. Today, anyone with a mobile phone or an internet-enabled computer is potentially under surveillance at any time. And information about political 'subversives' is widely shared between states.

- Criminalising whole sections of society through designating them 'illegal immigrants' – part of the process of controlling the precarious and the surplus, and thereby enabling higher levels of exploitation and oppression.
- The growing use of facial-recognition software in political repression. With the use of CCTV cameras plus facial recognition, police in many countries can know who is at a particular demonstration or other radical action in real time. Data collection on 'subversives' is ubiquitous and routine.

Pointing out the increasing use of repression to maintain social control is not to imply that in some past liberal-democratic utopia it did not exist. It is to say that there has been a qualitative shift from consent to coercion, towards the militarisation of social control on a global scale, especially since the 2008 financial crash and the onset of sustained neoliberal crisis.

Prisoners of the American Dream

In the United States, police-military repression has been used since the end of the American Civil War to enforce the segregation and subordination of the Black population. This has involved a combination of violent policing and the racial stereotyping of Black people, especially Black youth. The result is a prison system where 40% of prisoners are Black and more than 20% Latino.

In his 1987 book *Prisoners of the American Dream*, Mike Davis says that the American capitalist class has maintained itself in power by repression, and by its continued ability to divide the working class on the basis of 'race' and ethnicity. Historically, this was English against Irish, English and Irish against Germans, and all Whites against all Blacks. Today, the dominant forms of US racism are anti-Black, anti-Latino, anti-Muslim, and anti-migrant.

Racial discrimination plus police-prison repression keeps working-class Black Americans 'in their place'. The war against so-called 'illegal immigrants' plays the same role in relation to the Latino population, and this has spawned a huge network of border guards and immigration enforcement officers – a total of around 40,000.

The response of Donald Trump and his allies to the 2020 Black Lives Matter uprising shows two things about the ideology of fear around which many people in comfortable white middle-class suburbs, but also, regrettably, millions of white working-class people, can be mobilised. First is the use of the term 'terrorism' in relation to the protests, conjuring up images of bombing, shooting, and mayhem. Second is the ideological stereotyping of the Black population. Put together, it says 'the barbarians are at the gate, but don't worry, I'm your law-and-order President'.

A similar labelling of political opponents as 'terrorists' is on full display in the battle for democracy in Hong Kong. It has long been a government tactic in Erdoğan's Turkey (where political support for Kurdish independence is automatically 'terrorist'), and has been used repeatedly by Vladimir Putin against Chechen rebels and others. China has also justified its mass incarceration of the Uighur population in Xian-Jiang province, where more than a million people are held in concentration camps, as being part of the war against terrorism.

Terrorism, the war on drugs, illegal immigration, sedition: all these have been used worldwide to justify the paramilitarisation of policing. This is so ubiquitous in the United States that it is often difficult to tell whether the forces of law and order are police, National Guard, or Army.

US police departments having a huge array of hardware stems in part from the decision after the 2003 Gulf War to sell off surplus military equipment to them cheaply, so that even some small towns received automatic rifles, Humvees, desert combat uniforms, and sometimes armoured cars and helicopters. This, combined with the macho gun culture prevalent in the States, encourages aggressive and ultra-violent police behaviour during protests, drug raids, and even routine patrolling.

Militarised accumulation

The idea of the Global Police State encompasses two other key developments. First is what William I Robinson calls 'militarised accumulation'. The needs of expanded armed forces, border guards, intelligence agencies, and riot squads has made arms production and military employment and supply a giant factor in the world economy. Vast state expenditure on the armed forces, the police, the prisons, and the borders involves a recycling of tax revenues and government debt into corporate contracts.

Military production companies like Lockheed Martin, Northrop Grumman, and BAE Systems are among the most profitable in the world. These in turn are deeply integrated with hi-tech companies, which also take a share of the vast military budgets, financing increasingly digitalised military platforms and warfare techniques. These have been developed in particular in anticipation of future conflict with China.

A further dimension of the Global Police State is its intersection with growing far-right and neo-fascist forces. In the United States this includes gun culture and a celebration of militarism. The fascist armed groups that participated in anti-lockdown demonstrations in mid 2020 were often dressed in military-style uniforms and carried army-style weapons, with no attempt by the police to intervene. This is no longer the preserve of a few crank survivalists and Nazi mini-cults. As Henry A Giroux points out:

For the last 40 years, the United States has pursued a ruthless form of neoliberalism that has stripped economic activity from ethical considerations and social costs. One consequence has been the emergence of a culture of cruelty in which the financial elite produce inhuman policies that treat the most vulnerable with contempt… Under the Trump administration, the repressive state and market apparatuses that produced a culture of cruelty in the 19th century have returned with a vengeance, producing new levels of harsh aggression and extreme violence in US society.

After the crash: post-crisis repression

In the world after the 2008 financial crash, global austerity provoked a huge outpouring of protest which was violently repressed in states across the world. The riot police became a fixture of nightly TV news bulletins. Right-wing governments used water cannon, rubber bullets, tear gas, and – on occasion – more lethal methods to suppress anti-austerity protestors. And in many countries laws were changed to make it more difficult to hold legal protests.

For radical critics of the system this was no surprise. Since the publication of the English version of his *Prison Notebooks* in 1976, the ideas of Italian Marxist Antonio Gramsci, and particularly his notion of 'hegemony', have swept the radical Left. Simply put, this says that the capitalist class stays in power by a combination of state repression and ideological dominance. The consent, open or tacit, of a majority of people most of the time is achieved through ruling-class domination of the press, TV, the education system, churches, and, today, online media.

In fact, until the 2000 Millennium, the idea of ruling-class cultural and political hegemony held more sway in left-wing explanations of capitalism's durability than the repression of police, courts, and prisons. After all, in most advanced capitalist countries, and sporadically in others, protest was tolerated.

After the 2008 crisis the balance changed, with an avalanche of police and military violence. This is unsurprising. During the post-war boom in advanced capitalist countries after 1948, workers' income and consumption increased significantly. But as economic crises multiplied and incomes stagnated after 1973, social peace eroded and conflict between the state and employers on one side, and workers and other oppressed people on the other, intensified.

Episodically in this period, repression was used in heavy doses against major struggles. Police violence during 1984-5 British miners' strike was a key factor in its defeat, coupled with anti-union laws that have progressively made it more and more difficult to hold legal strikes in Britain. And police-military violence was used at massive levels in the United States in the 1960s, first against Civil Rights protests in the South, then against Black rebellions and riots in the North.

But with the fightback against austerity after the 2008 economic crisis, repression became more generalised and sustained. The French Yellow Vest movement in 2018-19 was met with levels of violence that led to dozens being blinded, losing hands, and in a few cases becoming paralysed. The French CRS riot police also mobilised armoured cars and a full spectrum of semi-military equipment. In America, huge resources are put into intelligence agencies and surveillance. Prison sentences are harsh and 2.3 million people are locked up in American prisons, many serving absurdly long sentences. And the increasing militarisation of the American state, with vast numbers employed in the Army, Marines, Navy, and Air Force, and the trillions spent on weaponry, have led to a new version of the Cold War 'permanent arms economy'. The United States, moreover, is internationalising the role of its police forces, particularly the FBI, linking them with the repressive agencies of allied states, pushing towards an integrated Global Police State.

Prior to the Covid-19 pandemic, which has knocked all economies off their axes, military spending in the US in particular has been a key factor in boosting and stabilising capitalist economies. Seemingly disconnected phenomena, like repression of 'illegal' immigrants, the development of weaponry to be used in outer space, and the militarisation of domestic police forces, are in fact linked to a turn by the increasingly internationalised capitalist class towards repression and violence, not just to create domestic and international order, but as part of the basis for further capital accumulation.

The Spanish state: collapsing democracy

What has happened in Spain is symbolic because, following the collapse of the fascist regime after Franco's death in 1976, the country was regarded as one of the most democratic and open in the world. Nothing could be censored and no demonstration banned, as the country moved towards elections in 1978.

After the economic crisis of 2008, nowhere was the anti-austerity movement deeper than in Spain, leading to a huge mass movement of predominantly young people – the Indignados, meaning, roughly, the 'Outraged'.

Spanish youth had much to be outraged about. Spain has had one of the highest unemployment rates in Europe, reaching a Eurozone record of 21.3%. The total number of unemployed people stood at 4,910,200 at the end of March 2011, when the youth unemployment rate was 43.5%, the highest in the European Union.

The protests kicked off in September 2010 when the main trade unions called a general strike against government plans for a sweeping overhaul of labour laws – designed to make it easier to fire workers and removing legal protection on pay and conditions.

In May 2011, a massive anti-austerity movement erupted, usually taking the form of the open-air occupations of major plazas or open spaces in front of town halls. As the protests became larger in the run-up to the general election, the electoral commission tried to ban the protests. In June, police attacks on demonstrators multiplied. Ruth Simsa comments:

> *From 2011 onwards, repression of activists has been observed with a rise in financial penalties, the misuse of existing laws, and police violence. The interior ministry increased public spending on anti-riot equipment. While Spain was called to order several times for police torture before the rise of social activism by the European Union, police brutality now rose. Amnesty International has documented incidents of police violence against protesters, including the use of clubs and rubber bullets.*

The government reacted with new laws on public security and 'terrorism', and a reform of the criminal code, ratified in July 2015, to impose restrictions on civil-society activists and reduce the rights of freedom of assembly and freedom of expression. This included repressive measures of breathtaking anti-democratic content, including fines of up to €600,000 for unauthorised demonstrations. The new laws forbade the photographing or filming of police officers in situations where doing so could 'put them in danger'. This could result in a fine of up to €30,000. Showing a 'lack of respect' to those in uniform, meanwhile, could mean a fine of €600.

The turn to repression was on full show in October 2017, when the government in Madrid sent thousands of riot police from the *Guardia Civil* to Catalonia to try to disrupt the independence referendum called by the province's nationalist leaders for that day. More than 800 people were injured in the resulting clashes. Shocking scenes of police manhandling and beating old and young alike sullied Spain's reputation worldwide. Two years later, in October 2019, Spanish courts handed out sentences of up to 13 years to the leaders of the Catalan independence movement.

The police repression of youth, worker protests, and the Catalan independence movement had an important political consequence. While the *Indignados* had provided the basis for the emergence of the *Podemos!* left-wing political party, the subsequent upsurge of state violence and attack on liberal-democratic norms was the context for the rise of Vox, a sinister fascist organisation that garnered substantial electoral support.

Erdoğan's Turkey: full-spectrum repression and creeping fascism
Turkey is an example of the full repertoire of political and police-military mobilisation to ensure the reactionary Right stays in power. Reactionary hegemony in Turkey depends on combining two things: first, the huge

mass base of Erdoğan's Justice and Development Party (AKP); and second, the step-by-step purge of the courts, the prison system, and the police, putting AKP loyalists in charge – and then using these self-same repressive apparatuses to crush opposition inside and outside the state.

Erdoğan trod the road used by many fascist and far-right leaders: that of winning power electorally in 2003, then attempting in successive waves to purge the state apparatus of opponents – the process the Nazis called *gleichschaltung*. Now Turkey, once considered a country with an increasingly 'modern' and democratic political system, has lurched into personal dictatorship and creeping fascism.

For the first 10 years of AKP government, huge amounts of foreign investment fuelled an economic boom. Things started to go wrong after the economic crash of 2008. Living standards stalled. At the same time there was a growing number of armed clashes with PKK (Kurdish Workers Party) guerrillas, and increasing tensions within the Islamist movement itself.

The storm broke when the 2013 Gezi Park movement shook the regime to its foundations. The occupation of the park in Istanbul to prevent its transformation into a giant shopping mall led to a massive pro-democracy movement that spread to dozens of urban centres, involving at various times up to 3.5 million people. This movement was violently repressed, with more than 20 deaths and hundreds of severe injuries among demonstrators.

Hard on the heels of the Gezi Park movement, PKK supporters in the Kurdish south-east of the country began to declare their towns to be autonomous self-governing entities, which led to massive armed repression, the destruction of whole towns and villages, the death of around 5,000 people, and the imprisonment of many more. Thousands of Kurds from the region remain in jail.

After three years of growing turmoil, opponents of Erdoğan in the (traditionally secular-nationalist) Army and Air Force launched a military coup. This was easily defeated. Erdoğan proclaimed 'God has sent us this coup', and set about using the event as a pretext for the destruction of democracy.

More than 130,000 public employees were fired, including thousands of teachers and hundreds of police officers and judges. All opposition newspapers and TV channels have been shut down. Tens of thousands – a fifth of Turkey's 246,000-strong prison population – have been charged with 'terrorism' offences. Torture in jail is widespread.

While the left-wing and pro-Kurdish HDP party is banned, with all its leaders and tens of thousands of its members jailed, the moderate CHP party is able to participate in elections, and even won the mayoral election in Istanbul in 2018. It is unlikely, however, to be allowed to win any election that puts Erdoğan out of power.

Four 'wars' that bind military and police repression

There are four 'wars' or proto-wars that merge military and police repression. Each is led by the United States. The first is the vast war (or wars) in preparation – which may of course never take place – against China and/or Russia. This is dealt with below.

The others are the interlocking 'wars' against drugs, 'illegal' immigration, and 'terrorism'. These are used to legitimise the military interventions of the US and its allies in Asia, Africa, and Latin America, through which the United States establishes a military presence abroad and gets foreign states to march in lockstep with its objectives.

While conventional wars were continuing in Iraq and Afghanistan, the participation of US military personnel in anti-drugs operations in Latin America became a daily event. The war on drugs, originally stoked up by Ronald Reagan in the 1980s, has had dramatic domestic effects in the US. As Alfred McCoy points out:

> During the 1980s, President Ronald Reagan, a conservative
> Republican, dusted off Rockefeller's anti-drug campaign for
> intensified domestic enforcement, calling for a 'national crusade'
> against drugs and winning draconian federal penalties for
> personal drug use and small-scale dealing. For the previous 50
> years, the US prison population remained remarkably stable
> at just 110 prisoners per 100,000 people. The new drugs war,
> however, almost doubled those prisoners, from 370,000 in 1981
> to 713,000 in 1989. Driven by Reagan-era drug laws and parallel
> state legislation, prison inmates soared to 2.3 million by 2008,
> raising the country's incarceration rate to an extraordinary 751
> prisoners per 100,000 population. And 51% of those in federal
> penitentiaries were there for drug offenses.

McCoy points out that because of laws disenfranchising those convicted of a felony, nearly six million voters, most of them Black, are unable to cast their ballot. At the same time, rural areas with large prisons have an automatic constituency for the Republican Party among the guards and other prison workers.

The 'war on drugs' is blatant hypocrisy. Supplying its millions of affluent and respectable cocaine users, as well as millions of more miserable crack and heroin users lower down the social scale, the drug 'industry' provides hundreds of millions of dollars of 'hot' money laundered through US banks each year. Prohibition and the war on drugs knit together foreign military and political intervention with a major weapon of domestic and social control – one that justifies harsh policing of minority ethnic communities and the imprisonment of hundreds of thousands of Black people and Latinos.

The war on 'illegal' immigration combines attempts to control 'surplus' populations outside the core capitalist countries with the exploitation of cheap labour inside them. Immigrants on the periphery of Europe and on the Mexican border form a huge reserve pool of potentially very cheap labour. 'Illegal' immigrants can be made to take the worst, most insecure, lowest-paid jobs, and will be reluctant to organise (in unions) for fear of losing their jobs and/or being deported.

Border guards and immigration police are part of a vast interlocking network of security apparatuses, linked together through computerised surveillance systems, whose primary role is to control migrant labour. As William I Robinson and Xuan Santos explain:

> ... under capitalist globalisation a new global immigrant labour supply system has come to replace earlier direct colonial and racial caste controls over labour worldwide... The rise of new systems of transnational labour mobility and recruitment have made it possible for dominant groups around the world to reorganise labour markets and recruit transient labour forces that are disenfranchised and easy to control.

> Then there is the ongoing 'war against terror'. This provides further opportunity for large-scale US military intervention around the world, for operations to clear the ground for capital accumulation, and for all manner of highly profitable investment by the military-industrial-security complex.

> Each day, for example, US soldiers participate in an average of 80 anti-terrorist operations in Africa, mainly against the Islamists of Al-Shabaab in East Africa and Boko Haram in West Africa. You read that right: 80 operations a day in Africa alone. This brings us back to the central dynamic: the militarised repression and militarised accumulation of the Global Police State – whose flagship is the 'war on terror'.

The permanent arms economy

Since the First Gulf War in 1991, there has not been a single day that the world has been free from war. The promise of a 'peace dividend' following the fall of Communism and the end of the Cold War has proved to be wishful thinking.

This is not just a matter of foreign interventions by the United States: it involves dozens of states. In the First Gulf War, seven countries joined the coalition to reverse Saddam Hussein's annexation of Kuwait. More than 20 states have been involved in military action in Africa. A dozen countries were involved in the Second Gulf War (2003), and the insurgency that followed. An astonishing 61 countries sent military forces to participate in the US-led 'Enduring Freedom' operation – in reality 'Endless War' – in Afghanistan, beginning in 2001. And Russia has been involved in military operations in Chechnya, Georgia, and the Ukraine.

All told, the armies of more than 100 countries have been involved in external or internal wars since 1990. In fact, the fall of Communism facilitated an explosion of worldwide militarism on a scale not seen since the two world wars and the human catastrophes of the wars in Korea and Vietnam. One measure of the devastation is a 65% increase in the number of people worldwide displaced by violence in the last decade to a total of 70 million.

Liberal analysts tend to see war as 'external' to the economy and politics of the countries involved. They are wrong. Stepped-up militarism and war-fighting are a deliberate strategy with huge implications for the 'domestic' economy and political system. Militarism and war go hand-in-hand with appeals to nationalism, with reactionary politics more generally, with a strengthening of the Right and Far Right. Militarisation always impacts negatively on democracy. War and creeping fascism are twins.

The new militarism has given rise to a new 'permanent arms economy', just as the Cold War did in the 1950s. As William I Robinson explains:

> By the 21st century, the transnational capitalist class turned to several mechanisms in order to sustain global accumulation in the face of over-accumulation, above all, financial speculation in the global casino, along with the plunder of public finances, debt-driven growth and state-organised militarised accumulation...

> The crisis is pushing us toward a veritable global police state. The global economy is becoming ever more dependent on the development and deployment of systems of warfare, social control and repression, apart from political considerations, simply as a means of making profit and continuing to accumulate capital in the face of stagnation. The so-called wars on drugs and terrorism; the undeclared wars on immigrants, refugees, gangs, and poor, dark-skinned and working-class youth more generally; the construction of border walls, immigrant jails, prison-industrial complexes, systems of mass surveillance, and the spread of private security guard and mercenary companies, have all become major sources of profit-making.

> The events of September 11, 2001, marked the start of an era of a permanent global war in which logistics, warfare, intelligence, repression, surveillance, and even military personnel are more and more the privatised domain of

> *transnational capital. Criminalisation of surplus humanity activates state-sanctioned repression that opens up new profit-making opportunities for the transnational capitalist class. Permanent war involves endless cycles of destruction and reconstruction, each phase in the cycle fuelling new rounds of accumulation, and also results in the ongoing enclosure of resources that become available to the capitalist class...*

The scale of the militarised economy is stupendous. Worldwide it is close to two trillion dollars annually (that is two followed by twelve zeros). US expenditure is officially $748 billion, but some analysts claim it is nearer one trillion.

The United States, as well as being the world's leading consumer of military equipment and supplies, is also the main producer and exporter. The income and profits of its top defence companies are fabulous. Lockheed Martin's latest annual figures show an income of $45 billion, and the top ten defence contractors between them earned around $150 billion. This is the second most profitable sector of the US economy, next to the fabulously wealthy Apple and Microsoft. High-tech companies in the US earned about $400 billion all told.

But this is a misleading picture, in two ways. First, the US military is a major consumer of the hardware and software of the high-tech companies. Exact figures are hard to pin down, because the supply of IT products is often indirect, being supplies to major defence contractors like Lockheed Martin and Northrup Grumman.

Second, the list of suppliers to the US military is vast and goes way beyond the tanks, planes, missiles, and small-arms provided by defence contractors. The US military is a massive consumer of oil, food, transport, medical equipment, housing, clothing, construction equipment, telecommunications equipment, and so on. There are more than 800 US military bases worldwide, and 440 of them are in the United States itself. These have huge purchasing power in local communities. A US Army private earns an estimated $38,000 a year when allowances for housing and food and drink are factored in. Pay goes up substantially with years of service, and pay for officers is much higher.

The overall picture here is of a militarised sector that is a crucial part of the economy, employing millions of people, and re-cycling the economic surplus. It is a crucial factor in mitigating over-accumulation and attempting to stabilise the economy. Militarisation and the military are crucial factors in the political structure and economy of numerous countries worldwide, from Western Europe to the Middle East and East Asia.

Battlespace

US militarisation post-9/11 centred on trying to establish US leadership in a self-proclaimed 'war on terror'. This led to disastrous and endlessly expensive wars in Iraq and Afghanistan, and to US 'anti-terrorist' operations in many other countries, especially in Africa and the Arabian Peninsula.

While the 'war on terror' posture has been maintained, it has been coupled with the characterisation of China and Russia as enemy states. This highlights an uncomfortable contradiction inside the transnational capitalist class. While there is a growing integration of production between the United States and China – symbolised by the manufacture of most of Apple's products by the Chinese giant Foxconn – competition between the world's two largest capitalist countries nonetheless persists and intensifies. The Trump administration's campaign against the tech giant Huawei and its fake accusations of 'security risks' with the 5G mobile network was an example.

The fundamental strategic posture of the US military is preparation for possible war with China, with a subsidiary posture of possible wars with Russia, Iran, and the wretched victims of the 'war on terror' like Afghanistan and Iraq. This provides the ideological and political justification for a military structure of unprecedented size and complexity – the greatest concentration of 'means of destruction' in the history of humanity.

The key US military doctrine has shifted from the 'AirLand Battle'of the 1980s, aimed at Russia, to 'AirSea Battle' and 'Multi-Domain Dominance' in the last two decades, which envisages a massive and lethal assault on China, with a projected 20,000 dead per day.

Multi-Domain Dominance is an attempt to survey and control vast geographic areas, using cyber, electronic, and satellite platforms, which US defence wonks hope can be synthesised into an artificial-intelligence 'defence algorithm' capable of viewing a giant battlefield and selecting appropriate targets and tactics.

That requires an enormous array of new and highly expensive weaponry. In the early 1980s Mary Kaldor coined the phrase 'baroque arsenal' to refer to the huge potential overkill possessed by the US military under Reagan. Today's super-expensive actual and in-the-pipeline weapons might be referred to as 'super baroque'. Under Trump, at least until the coronavirus hit, all four services were getting exactly what they wanted, with price no object.

Hawk Carlisle, on the National Defence website, gives a glimpse of the information technology requirements involved:

> Potential adversaries are making significant improvements in cyber warfare in order to minimise traditional US dominance in all the other domains. The United States must become the best in cyber just as it has mastered all the other domains. This will require significant advancements by the US defence industrial base and the US military in new technologies like artificial intelligence, machine learning, autonomous and

semi-autonomous systems, quantum computing and big data, to name a few. Also, just as it understands and works to gain and maintain space, air, land, and naval superiority, it must also understand and work to gain and maintain superiority across the entire electromagnetic spectrum.

Surveillance capitalism: the global Panopticon

People looking for a particular product online may suddenly find advertisements for similar products on their email feed or Facebook page. That is because their internet usage is being tracked by a series of programmes, the most ubiquitous of which is called DoubleClick, owned by Google.

DoubleClick, which is hard to get rid of, builds an enormous database about users that alerts advertisers. This personal data is enormously valuable for Google, but an enormous invasion of personal privacy.

Supermarkets know everything about their customers' personal preferences by recording all debit card and online purchases, as do Amazon, Netflix, and other online retailers and entertainment providers. Every online movie a viewer has ever watched is recorded, for example, and what they watch gives away a lot about likely future consumer choices.

Marketing is a crucial feature of surveillance capitalism, and it is feeding an obsessive, neurotic, alienated kind of mass consumption, referenced in such colloquial phrases as 'retail therapy'. But that is not all: online behaviour also reveals political attitudes, and in a growing number of countries state spying on citizens though monitoring of their online (and mobile phone) activity is reaching epidemic levels.

Twenty or thirty years ago, trade unionists, socialist activists, peace campaigners, and dissidents of all sorts used to worry that their telephone calls were listened to and their mail opened by police and intelligence services. This did indeed take place on a large scale, and still does. But political surveillance is now mainly digitalised, and that has enabled a massive shift in both the quality and quantity of data collected.

A crucial part of contemporary surveillance is to intimidate people into not joining 'subversive' or critical activities, because of the likelihood that it will become known – at least to intelligence services and then potentially to employers or other authority figures.

The modern 'Panopticon' comprises a huge network of surveillance, with the United States (and its junior partner Britain), China, and Russia at its core. While Chinese electronic and internet surveillance is massive, especially of its own population, even China's massive efforts are dwarfed by the vast surveillance capabilities of the United States.

This was revealed by WikiLeaks' Edward Snowden, a former contractor for America's CIA spy agency, in 2013. He showed that America's National Security Agency (NSA) harvested vast amounts of data about the telephone conversations of millions of Americans, directly hacked into the databases of online and social media companies like Yahoo, Google, and Facebook, and tracked the phone conversations of foreign political leaders, including allegedly 'friendly' ones like Germany's Angela Merkel.

The United States is plugged into a global system of surveillance with its Anglophone allies – the UK, Australia, New Zealand, and Canada – through the so-called 'Five Eyes Intelligence Alliance'. It has also forged similar links with European states and companies.

Through all these programmes the internet has been turned into a vast surveillance network, instantly available and usable by police and intelligence networks. It is not just the sites people visit; it is the built-in cameras of their lap-tops that can be used any time to watch them.

Now surveillance has morphed into real time, following individuals through their smart phones. China, which has thousands of desk-based agents monitoring its own citizens, leads the world in this technology. It is using the Covid pandemic to roll out tracking apps that will tell the authorities where people are, where they have been, who they have been meeting. The dictatorship also has 200 million CCTV cameras in place, and makes extensive use of facial-recognition software.

Surveillance and data are crucial and interlinked in three dimensions in modern capitalism – marketing, political and police surveillance, and military operations.

The US military's Multi-Domain Dominance strategy, paralleled by other leading military states like China and Russia, depends on vast amounts of data and 'battlespace' surveillance. The choice of the Lockheed's F-35 as the main combat aircraft for US forces, as opposed to apparently near-identical competitors like the F-22 Raptor, is not due to its superior capacity in dogfights with Russian and Chinese planes. It is because the F-35 is really a flying super-computer with the ability to survey and track vast areas, and to deliver powerful missiles against multiple targets.

In the next chapter, we explore how the architecture of the capitalist internet has given rise not only to new forms of surveillance, but also interacted with the increasingly proletarianised and atomised reactionary middle strata of some societies to produce a unique new social base for fascism. Moreover, online fascism makes direct use of internet surveillance – as when the far-right political consultancy firm Cambridge Analytica misappropriated data to help reactionary causes in 2016's UK Brexit referendum and US presidential election, but also earlier in the 2014 US midterm elections, and elsewhere, in Australia, India, Kenya, Malta, and Mexico.

After the virus

How will coronavirus and lockdown impact on the global slide towards militarisation and police-state repression? That will depend on the struggles that are bound to develop as neoliberal regimes impose new austerity and crackdown and the world economy collapses into depression and mass unemployment. Around the world, ruling classes are preparing for escalating class warfare.

Numerous states have passed laws giving extensive anti-democratic authority to those in power. In Hungary it is now a criminal offence to spread 'misinformation' about coronavirus, and Prime Minister Viktor Orbán can rule by decree for an indefinite period. In Britain and other countries, new powers to detain people on suspicion of 'terrorism' have been passed. It remains to be seen whether these powers will be used any time soon: the important thing is that they are there. Past experience shows these kinds of laws, passed for a temporary emergency, often become permanent.

The crisis is making intrusive policing normal. The military are seen on the streets as a matter of course in many countries, and police have unlimited powers to ask people why they are out of their homes. These powers are justified by the claim that they are necessary to enforce lockdowns, but they are likely to be retained in 'the new abnormal' following the pandemic.

The role of the military is being swivelled towards domestic tasks in countries that do not have a history of such interference in civil affairs. For the moment this has usually been to augment medical responses, by carrying out tests, delivering supplies, and dealing with corpses, but it has also involved troops in countries like Britain, France, Germany, and Italy patrolling streets and beaches and checking motorists.

The virus is also being used to impose intrusive new surveillance techniques that will enable the state to track the population.

What comes of these trends will depend on the struggle from below over the next decade. What is clear is that, in the context of neoliberal capitalism's deep, worsening, and perhaps terminal crisis, the increasingly militarised state – the Global Police State – represents a mortal threat to democracy. It is the embodiment of a creeping fascism that threatens us all.

Chapter 6

The New Fascism

On 3 November 2020, far right US President Donald Trump was defeated at the polls. During the following week, it looked as if he and his supporters in the Republican Party and beyond might attempt to overturn the results and carry out a judicial-political coup, perhaps using the right-wing majority in the Supreme Court to invalidate the votes in several states. Eventually, though, the gap in the popular vote between Trump and Biden was too large, and the street mobilisation of his stunned supporters too weak, for it to be a runner.

Trump's huge mobilisations of support in mass rallies, his brutal governmental style, his support in the right-wing media, all seemed suddenly to count for nothing. Had it all been an aberration, an illusion of threatened dictatorship and modern fascism? Can we now expect a return to democratic 'normality'?

Actually, the reverse is true. The Far Right and creeping fascism – on the streets, at the polls, in government, in police departments – are not going away. Not in the US and not around the world. That is because it is rooted in the capitalist crisis and the political polarisation that are eroding the foundations of 'moderate' centrist liberal-parliamentary rule across the world.

Supporters of the centre in the US and Britain imagine that the extremist demon has been vanquished. *Guardian* columnist Jonathan Freedland wrote: 'It's clearer every day that in electing Biden and rejecting Donald Trump, Americans are moving to undo the great error they made in 2016.'

But are they? Was Trump just an 'error' of judgement. Can such unfortunate mistakes now be avoided? Is it all that simple?

In the last decade, there has been an astonishing rise of the Far Right and fascism internationally, starting well before the Trump bid for the US presidency. Thirty years after Francis Fukuyama's famous *End of History* predicted that, with the fall of the Soviet Union, capitalism and democracy would be victorious everywhere, the balance sheet is in: capitalism has been victorious – an exceptionally predatory, destructive, anti-social brand of it – but democracy has not. On the contrary, a modern form of fascism has emerged, re-enacting the racist, xenophobic, and nationalist themes of the Nazi and pro-Nazi movements of the 1930s.

How could this have happened? How could the neoliberal world created by Margaret Thatcher and Ronald Reagan in the 1980s under the banner of 'freedom' have given rise to historical monsters in the form of Donald Trump, Brazilian President Jair Bolsonaro, and Turkish President Recep Tayyip Erdoğan? How could we end up with thousands of desperate migrants drowning in the Mediterranean Sea, and armed fascist militias patrolling the streets of large American cities?

The key to understanding this lies in the form of capital's victory in the 1980s and 1990s. As explained in Chapters 3 and 7, the neoliberal world created by Thatcher and Reagan produced a deeply dysfunctional economic system that devastated the lives of billions of people across the world. Then the 2008 financial crash – a direct consequence of the permanent debt economy created by neoliberal policy – was followed by programmes of austerity that ratcheted up the social crisis to a new intensity. In Paul Mason's words, rebellion 'kicked off everywhere' – in the United States and Greece, in Turkey and Britain, across the Arab world, and in dozens of countries around the globe.

Sections of the capitalist class re-learned an obvious lesson: you cannot keep social desperation and mass rebellion in check over long periods of time simply by repression. Something more popular than riot police and soldiers on the streets are needed to stabilise the social order – an ideology capable of heading off popular revolt against the bankers, the rich, and the system by turning mass anger onto other targets.

This has been the context for Donald Trump, the Vox party in Spain, the Lega in Italy, the *Allianz für Deutschland* (Alliance for Germany, AfD), Bolsonaro in Brazil, and numerous other far-right movements worldwide

The crisis of capitalist democracy

The stability of capitalist democracy after World War II was built on relative economic prosperity and rising living standards. Destroy prosperity and welfare systems, and capitalist democracy, one way or another, is liable to flounder and collapse.

Robert Kutzer, in his book *Can Democracy Survive Global Capitalism?*, answers his own question in the negative. More precisely he says:

Democratic capitalism today is a contradiction in terms. Globalisation under the auspices of finance-capital has steadily undermined the democratic constraints on capitalism. In a downward spiral, popular revulsion against predatory capitalism has strengthened populist ultra-nationalism and weakened democracy.

Because Kuttner is a social-democrat, he poses the issue as controlled capitalism versus authoritarian dictatorship. We pose the choices differently. Like his mentor Karl Polanyi, Kuttner sees the Far Right as much better able to benefit from economic crisis and social collapse than the Left. This is because the Far Right defends the power and prerogatives of capital, while the Left faces endless hostility from the defenders of the system, including right-wing and centrist politicians and mainstream media. Political polarisation is therefore liable, in the first instance at least, to benefit mainly the Far Right.

Kuttner is surely right about neoliberal capitalism and democracy. It is not just a matter of undermining democratic rights of demonstration and assembly. It is about destroying every form of dissent and resistance. This involves ending public ownership and control, manipulating and rigging elections, attacking public-service broadcasting and critical media, purging the universities of radical teachers and content, and privatising national and local government functions so they escape popular oversight. This process inevitably leads to widespread corruption, and the dictators are often themselves immensely rich and self-serving (Turkey's Erdoğan, Russia's Vladimir Putin, and China's Xi Jinping are all billionaires).

So the first part of our argument is that the massive and intractable crises we face are, in the long term, incompatible with capitalist democracy. This should not surprise us. Capitalist democracy has existed for a much shorter time than capitalism itself. Francis Fukuyama's prediction that capitalist globalisation would lead to the victory of democracy everywhere has proved wrong on all counts.

The second part of our argument is that simple repression is rarely sufficient to defeat popular resistance. It is also necessary to build a mass reactionary base. This is the genius of the project of Turkish President Recep Tayyip Erdoğan. He has used the mass electoral base of the Islamist AKP Party as his route to power, and then used his presidential position and parliamentary majority to successively purge the police, the army, the judiciary, the civil service, and the universities of all opponents and possible opponents in a classic process of *gleichschaltung* – literally 'synchronisation', the German word used to describe how the Nazis gradually bent the existing apparatuses of the state to their will after Hitler became Chancellor in 1933. Combined with this, Erdoğan has engineered the most brutal repression of all popular movements, especially the Kurdish-led People's Democratic Party (HDP). Tens of thousands have been killed, hundreds of thousands jailed, many tortured, raped, and otherwise brutalised.

Robert Kuttner brands both Erdoğan's Turkey and Putin's Russia as 'soft fascism', because although some of the forms of democracy, like managed elections, continue, these are rendered largely meaningless in practice. There are differences: Erdoğan has a mass party of immense power behind him (the AKP has 11 million members), whereas Putin's United Russia (two million members) relies much more on the central state apparatus itself. But these are differences of degree, not type.

There are obvious differences, too, with interwar fascism. In the 1930s, a mass reactionary electoral base backed up armies of street-fighters needed to physically defeat the Left and the workers' movement on the streets. Nowadays, the surveillance state and militarised police forces have relegated armed fascist militias to a secondary role.

Central to our argument is that the existing state is the primary instrument of fascist-type repression. Fascism has never come to power by overthrowing the existing capitalist state, only ever by winning state power – by both legal/electoral and illegal/extra-parliamentary methods – and then bending that power to its own purposes. This was even true of the most extreme version of fascism, the Nazis in Germany. Socialism involves the revolutionary overthrow of the existing state; fascism does not. In most cases, existing police and military forces can be used to crush the Left and the popular movements.

Creeping fascism defeated?

The economic and social crisis that creates the opportunity for the Far Right and the slide towards fascism creates a polarisation. Everywhere, there is mass resistance.

The most dramatic example in 2020, in the United States and internationally, was the Black Lives Matter movement, which had the active support of millions – workers, oppressed people, young people – and which, of course, was met with vicious state repression and involved head-to-head confrontations with armed fascist militias.

The last part of 2020 also saw: an upsurge of rebellion against the far-right regime in Poland, led by young women and focused especially on resisting new anti-abortion attacks; the sweeping left victory in the referendum in Chile, aimed at ditching a constitution that enshrines privatisation and neoliberalism; the return to power of the Movement Towards Socialism (MAS) in Bolivia; and an exceptionally militant uprising against corruption and repression in Peru.

Karl Polanyi tended to pose the alternatives as liberalism or fascism. More precisely, he argued, if the liberals and social-democrats do not introduce regulated capitalism, then the fascists will come to power. If that is the real choice, we are in trouble, because the aftermath of the

2008 crash showed clearly that liberals and social-democrats are not prepared to challenge the prerogatives of capital; in or out of power, they stick with neoliberal austerity. More than that: they continually attempt to head off the fascists and the Far Right by stealing their clothes, especially on immigration.

The main recent exception, of course, was the Jeremy Corbyn movement in the Labour Party. The campaign against him waged by the capitalist class and its allies on the right of the Labour Party was really about his radical programme. Bernie Sanders in the United States was also a partial exception; and he too was the recipient of fierce hostility from the capitalist class and the right-wing of the Democrats.

The emerging forces of rebellion – workers, the youth, women, minorities – are the basis of a real alternative, that of anti-capitalist revolution. The stakes really are that high. We are not going back to the 1970s or the 1950s: either we open up the road to anti-capitalist transition or we risk fascism, militarisation, and ecological and social collapse.

A vivid example of the sustained danger of creeping fascism is the growth of Vox in the Spanish state. Vox has built itself out of opposition to the national demands of Spain's regions, in particular the Catalan demand for independence. The party raps itself in the colours of reactionary Castilian nationalism. It has highly reactionary positions on women (defending soldiers accused of gang rape, for example) and promotes dog-whistle homophobia. It self-consciously resumes the tradition of former dictator Francisco Franco in its Catholicism and xenophobic nationalism. It has stolen most of the electoral base of the allegedly middle-of-the-road *Ciudadanos* (Citizens) party. Now it is trying to put itself at the head of anti-lockdown demonstrations in Madrid and elsewhere. Regrettably it has, by clever use of social media, won a base among young people.

It is impossible to analyse parties like Vox with a template derived from the 1930s, checking for similarities with and differences from Nazism to decide whether or not they are 'fascist'. Vox is a modern analogue of 1930s fascism. It is a movement in process, and its dynamic and programme is towards the crushing of capitalist democracy; it is one variant among many of creeping fascism.

War on socialism

It was no surprise that during the US presidential election the Cuban-American population of Florida was showered with anti-socialist messages by the Trump campaign. Mainly this is a reactionary ex-patriate community, consumed with hatred of the Communist government in Cuba and, more recently, of the Chavist regime in Venezuela.

But the Republican onslaught on 'socialism' went much further. In his acceptance speech at the Republican convention, Donald Trump said: 'This election will decide whether we save the American Dream or whether we allow a socialist agenda to demolish our cherished destiny.'

Throughout the US election campaign, attacks on socialism were constant, as were attempts to paint Biden and Obama as socialists in league with Cuba and Venezuela. The content of these attacks was absurd – Biden and Obama have nothing to do with socialism – but the very fact of this discourse is significant.

What is glided over in the discussion is the difference between socialism, social-democracy, and liberalism – that is, respectively, between the revolutionary transformation of society, a substantial programme of social reform, and limited government action on things like health, welfare, and the environment. Non-socialist Democrats like Biden and Obama fall, at best, into the latter category.

On the other hand, in the United States, recent polls show majorities, especially in the 18-34 and over 55 age groups, with a positive image of socialism, as opposed to capitalism. Many of these people probably have in mind state-regulated welfare capitalism on the European model. But the hostility to actually existing capitalism is significant – and dangerous for the ruling class.

The attack on 'socialism' in the US is a pre-emptive campaign against the emergence of a hardened socialist and class-struggle opposition to neoliberalism and the Far Right – against the sort of politics represented by growing union militancy, mass BLM protests, and the Democratic Socialists of America.

The fascist and semi-fascist forces are far from finished in the United States. They include a range of forces from the Republican Party to the tens of thousands of members of armed right-wing militias. In the present period of endless crisis it is unlikely that these forces will disappear. It is unlikely that Trump himself will quietly leave the stage. The hard-right politics of Trumpism will probably continue to dominate the Republican Party, providing an extremely powerful echo-chamber for far-right mobilisation.

An immediate focus may be the campaign to overturn the Supreme Court's 1973 Roe-versus-Wade judgment that legalised abortion across the country. In this case, the Far Right will be able to draw on America's massive reserves of Christian reaction, mainly Evangelical, but also Catholic.

Europe: waiting in the wings

The rise of the Far Right in Europe has been particularly shocking, for this was the continent that gave rise to the Nazis and the Holocaust. Modern fascism does not re-enact the symbolism and street-fighting militias of the Nazis. Parties like the French *Rassemblement National* and the *Alternative für Deutschland* (AfD) present themselves as mainstream organisations but with a strong line on nationalism and immigration. But they all have a hard fascist core.

They aim to come to power through the ballot box. But what happens when they do is vividly demonstrated by events in Hungary since Viktor Orbán and his Fidesz party assumed power in 2010. Orbán calls his system 'national co-operation', a phrase eerily similar to the 'national consolidation' demanded by 1930s fascists.

Hungary shares many features with the 'soft fascism' of Turkey. It has become a *de facto* one-party state. The electoral law has been gerrymandered so that in the 2014 elections Fidesz won 44% of the vote and 66% of the seats in the national parliament. The media has been brought to heel, either closed down or consolidated into the Press and Media Foundation, effectively a pro-government cartel. The judiciary has been intimidated and purged. Opposition media, parties, and NGOs face arbitrary tax demands.

Government contracts increasingly go to Orbán's family and friends. Like most authoritarian regimes, Hungary under Fidesz is riddled with corruption and theft of public funds.

This mix of authoritarianism and crony capitalism is topped with an ideology that Orbán calls 'illiberal democracy' – with nationalism, anti-migrant and anti-Roma racism, and rampant antisemitism to build and sustain a reactionary electoral base. Hungary is now deep into the process of *gleichschaltung*, with some of the forms of democracy maintained, but, in reality, a one-party dictatorship.

In Italy, Germany, and France, the far-right parties – the Lega, the AfD, and the *Rassemblement National* – are not currently in government, but they are all powerful political forces. They have not gone away. They are waiting in the wings. The fall of Donald Trump will not stymie them. And support for them is being fed by the liberal and social-democratic centre.

Nothing could demonstrate this more starkly than the anti-Muslim outbursts of French President Emmanuel Macron following the gruesome murder of schoolteacher Samuel Paty by an Islamist terrorist in November 2020. Macron's attack on French Muslims has been reminiscent of attacks on French Jews by Second World War president and Nazi collaborator Marshal Philippe Pétain. Macron's threat of restrictions against, and policing of, Muslim communities and their religious practices echoes the demands of *Rassemblement National* leader Marine Le Pen. Far from 'outflanking' Le Pen, the effect is to endorse her politics.

Migrants and Muslims: the 'Jews' of modern fascism
We have argued that fascism and the Far Right represent a distinct response to the crisis by sections of the ruling class eager to undercut the class-struggle alternative. But dig deeper and we discover the presence of right-wing forces whose long years of ideological warfare and organisation are now bearing fruit in the new faces of fascism.

The first of these are the small fascist organisations themselves, which have never gone away, even if they have changed their political clothes several times. An example is the *Fratelli d'Italia* (Brothers of Italy), the junior brother to the Lega party in the Italian electoral Far Right. The Brothers of Italy are the re-baptised form of the Italian Social Movement (MSI), founded immediately after the Second World War to uphold the tradition of Benito Mussolini. Other major European parties of the Far Right, like the *Rassemblement National* (formerly National Front) in France, the AfD in Germany, and *Vlaams Belang* (formerly *Vlaams Blok*) in Belgium, all have a hard core connected in one way or another with the old fascist tradition.

Fascist and semi-fascist movements need high-profile issues around which to build support. The most important of these is, of course, anti-migrant racism and xenophobia. This is the cutting-edge of a broader ideological attack on multiculturalism, seen as an ideological flagship of the Left.

The anti-multiculturalist turn is rooted in Islamophobia, defence of the 'Judaeo-Christian' West, seen as the crux of world civilisation and progress. The fight against multiculturalism was taken up by British-American academic Bernard Lewis and his student Samuel Huntington. Lewis originated the notion of 'the Clash of Civilisations', stressing the alleged centuries-long battle between Islam and Christianity. Huntington popularised this idea, adding 'Confucian civilisation' (i.e. China) as a third element in the mix.

For Lewis and Huntington, Islam represents an instinctively imperialist ideology bent on world domination. It is no wonder then that Lewis and especially Huntington became world famous after the 9/11 attacks in Washington and New York. The caricature of Muslims as the uncivilised 'other' was deepened in the West by the so-called 'war on terror'. The Anglo-American attacks on Afghanistan and Iraq had a massive impact in news media and political debate.

Online fascism

Technology was in the backdrop of interwar fascism, shadowed by a world war that unleashed a carnage previously only latent in modernity. Some fascists, the Italian Futurists, aesthetically lauded such horrors. Innovation – for good and ill – has not since ceased; it continues to change the social and political world, including fascism.

The internet is both fast-moving (giddyingly frictionless) and, counter-intuitively, a perfect time capsule (preserving all it touches). The strangeness of such a 'fast fixity' adds to an impression that 'virtual' cyberspace is immaterial, less real than the world. Everything is throwaway, but, on the other hand, online-time's detritus proves eternally recoverable.

Today's 'human dust' (Trotsky's term for interwar fascism's mass base) hunches over computers anonymously bemoaning their neoliberal proletarianisation. Both skilled, unionised, well-paid jobs in industry and stable white-collar jobs in the service sector have been exported to the

Global South. Oppressed, marginalised, often migrant minorities pick up low-wage jobs that no-one else wants. This has produced a distinctly neoliberal hyper-alienation, whose victims struggle to process their new precarity. Meanwhile, 'the shit of ages' (Marx's term for the reactionary cocktail of right-wing politics) is uploaded, digitised to flow freely through a leaky online sewage system.

Alienated millennials, raised online and on the meritocratic fantasies of a 90s bubble economy – falsely promised they would enjoy better lives than their relatively privileged parents – find in recovered prejudices the scapegoats for their diminished circumstances. Ancient hatreds are thereby given web 2.0 twists.

The so-called 'manosphere' illustrates this. At its core, the 'men's rights movement' (MRM) perceive 'misandry' (the opposite of misogyny) in gendered social problems (higher rates of criminalisation and suicide among men, for example). And while racialised misandries do exist – for instance, directed at Black American men – MRM is in fact misdiagnosing the toll class society's patriarchy takes even on men; as well documented by feminist theory. However, rather than turning to their true allies – feminists – they blame women.

This is the least obscene face of online misogyny. Deeper into the sewer we find. misanthropic incels (involuntary celibates) with their pseudoscience of female hypergamy (women forming relationships with men of higher social status), which at worst can inspire mass murder; the separatist 'Men Going Their Own Way' (MGTOW); and, at the other extreme, pick-up artists (PUAs), who encourage men to manipulate and cajole sex through techniques like 'negging' (i.e. emotional abuse).

The 'manosphere' overlaps alt-right and alt-lite subcultures, containing even more myriad subgroupings. The pseudo-philosophical Dark Enlightenment of Curtis 'Mencius Moldbug' Yarvin and Nick Land's imagining, for instance. Or neo-Nazis clustered around antisemitic conspiracies such as 'Cultural Bolshevism', which attributes Communism to a Jewish plot, repackaged as 'Cultural Marxism', i.e. the idea that Jewish Marxist academics conspire to corrupt the West with multiculturalism. Or the Boogaloo, who dream of apocalyptic violence, a mainstay of 80s Hollywood. Meanwhile, online far-right micro-celebrities and more mainstream right-wing political commentators (from white supremacist Richard Spencer to Fox's insidious Tucker Carlson) give a hipster or respectable veneer to fascist nostalgia.

Trump is not unique in drawing on the internet's power to motivate his social base, merely the most successful. From the Left, this was deliberately, if unsuccessfully, attempted by Jeremy Corbyn and Bernie Sanders. Tellingly, however, it was Ron Paul's 2008 Republican primary campaign – a racist, pro-border, pro-life, isolationist libertarian – who trialled social-media campaigning to draw in an online grassroots movement. His legacy fed directly into the online Far Right, with notables such as Spencer cutting their teeth with Paul's bid for the US presidency. Today, there is an entire ecology of far-right YouTube channels and podcasts, documented by grassroots anti-fascist journalism such as Daniel Harper and Jack Graham's podcast I Don't Speak German. As they explain, even 'alt-right' can be misleading. In the online world, coded language and labels constantly shift. Self-published ebooks, legions of amateur talk-shows droning as long as seven hours an episode, the latest murderer's manifesto, or a novel genre of racist memes, form a culture that – borne of 'fast fixity' – defies easy comprehension.

Different conspiracy theories are central to other fascist demographics online. The older 'boomer' fascists, unlike their millennial counterparts, waste time on Facebook (rather than Twitter and anonymous online boards) trading anti-vaxx or QAnon myths – positing a global paedophile network being fought by a heroic Trump. In the age of Covid, they find a leader in antisemitic conspiracy theorist David Icke; this contingent even contends that the pandemic is a fiction, an authoritarian plot to further the goal of mass micro-chipping and 5G implementation (re-imagined as a sinister technology that alters human brain-waves).

Since the 9/11 attacks, the trickle of increasingly bizarre conspiracy theories has become a torrent. Television shows in the 90s like The X-Files mainstreamed the idea of elaborate government plots (with episodes about vaccines used to track and trace). Later, less mainstream documentaries such as Zeitgeist: The Movie (2007) fixed these ideas. And after the Occupy demonstrations fractured, even some of the anti-capitalist movement joined in.

The superficial diversity of online ideas belies the fact that – serving the same counter-revolutionary ends – they always come back to the same old enemies (globalists, a code for Jews; metropolitan liberals; Muslims; the aggregated oppressed) and remedies (some return to an idealised past when powerful nation-states were corruption-free).The most extreme reactionaries deliberately blur themselves with naïve, more moderate associates (who might believe vaccines are dangerous, but not that George Soros encouraged Third-World migration to 'the West' in preparation for world government – an idea encouraged by mainstream far-right leaders Recep Tayyip Erdoğan, Viktor Orbán, and Donald Trump).

Fascism energises the middle strata of society and decayed sections of the working class as a defensive capitalist bulwark against mass resistance; its political function is to drain support from emancipatory projects and provide electoral fodder and shock-troops for reaction. This is why class collaboration is at fascism's core, and why it is both absurdly optimistic (a thousand-year Reich) and pessimistic (depicting oppressors as victims).

Filtered through the 'fast fixity' of the internet, fascist ideology has found new, dizzying obscenities, an organisational spontaneity, and a renewed capacity for fantasy. Badly cohered but difficult to identify, fragile (as demonstrated by the alt-right's collapse after the Unite the Right rally in Charlottesville, Virginia) but quickly regrouping (with a huge potential social base), online fascism is distinct and has shaped a culture war that revolutionary socialists must understand and overcome, rather than blithely ignore.

So what is fascism?

Fascism is a mass movement of the Right. It is the active mobilisation of reactionary class forces and atomised 'human dust' around the right-wing nexus of nationalism, racism, sexism, and authoritarianism. Fascism arises when capitalism is in crisis, and the property, power, and privilege of the ruling class is under threat.

The ruling class – the 1% – is a small minority. It rules through a mix of concession, consent, and coercion. Concessions are granted when the working class and the oppressed are on the offensive and it is necessary to assuage social discontent and stabilise the social order by addressing some of the injustices of class society. This helps to achieve consent, where sections of society are bought off, convinced of the legitimacy of the system, or at least persuaded that it cannot be changed; a way of marginalising and isolating any radical vanguard. Coercion, using the repressive state apparatus of army, police, prisons, courts, and surveillance, sometimes today reinforced by fascist auxiliaries, is necessary to crush mass resistance when it arises.

When the system is in crisis, and ever more people's lives are torn apart, united resistance from below becomes more likely. Mass unemployment, wage cuts, evictions, collapsing public services – especially when this contrasts with wealth and corruption at the top – leads to a 'crisis of legitimacy' for capitalism. The crisis limits the slack available for concessions. Consent withers. More coercion is necessary. 'Bobbies on the beat' become militarised riot police.

But social crisis combined with intensified state repression deepens the crisis of legitimacy. The system shits on you, then clubs you when you protest.

So consent, in one form or another, remains necessary – lest the entire mass of the working class, 85% of the population, rises as one against the system and overwhelms its repressive apparatus.

But consent can no longer be based on public well-being. The crisis means people's lives are getting worse, not better. Consent then becomes a matter of shifting the blame for social decay onto scapegoats. And because of the anger at lives falling apart, the scapegoat politics of the Right in a period of crisis become hyper-charged with rage. Here we find the inner core of fascism.

People who organise, mobilise, and fight as a collective force from below, in their own interests, against the system, against the real enemy, against the super-rich, the corporate profiteers, and the racist police state

– such people are drawn instinctively to left-wing ideas about solidarity, democracy, and equality.

But the atomised and alienated, those outside class-based forms of organisation, capitalism's 'human dust', are open to what Marx called 'the shit of ages' – the mass of prejudices and superstitions festering in the depths of capitalist society.

This social raw material can be fashioned into a counter-revolutionary mass movement to protect the system from the explosive potential inherent in society's accumulating discontents.

Formed of human dust, spewing the shit of ages, bloated with psychotic rage, fascism is a political mechanism by which a deeply dysfunctional, crisis-ridden system of exploitation and oppression generates social forces capable of smashing democracy, civil liberties, and any effective resistance to the rule of the rich and the corporations.

This inner essence is common to both 'first-wave' interwar fascism and 'second-wave' creeping fascism today. But there are differences of form. This was true, of course, in the 1930s. There were notable differences between Italian Fascism, German Nazism, Japanese Militarism, and Spanish Nationalism; and further differences with fascism in Austria, Hungary, Romania, Vichy France, and elsewhere. The variety of forms in which fascism appears is equally apparent today.

We can identify four main components of contemporary fascism: the role of far-right parties in building a mass reactionary electoral bloc; the role of the internet in disseminating far-right propaganda and in creating, consolidating, and mobilising the fascist core; the role of the bourgeois state, especially increasingly militarised police, in the implementation of authoritarian and nationalist-racist policies, and in the repression of popular movements; and the role of fascist militias and mobs as auxiliaries.

To return to Robert Kuttner's question: can democracy survive global capitalism? Our answer is no. In the long term, the road to fascism and reaction remains open as long as an anti-capitalist alternative is not built. And that alternative can only be built by direct confrontation with the major weapons of division deployed by the fascists and the Far Right— racism, homophobia, transphobia, misogyny, xenophobia. It is only in that fight that we can shut the door to a repeat of the fascist disaster of the 1930s.

Chapter 7

The Economics of Disaster Capitalism

The only questions concerned the trigger and the timing. Neoliberalism is the most dysfunctional and parasitic form of capitalism in the history of the system. It is characterised by economic stagnation, financial speculation, grotesque and growing inequality, trillions of dollars of waste expenditure, and a repeating cycle of boom, bubble, and bust. Striding the world in pursuit of corporate profit, it leaves in its wake social, ecological, and military devastation.

It was only a matter of how and when. The trigger turned out to be Covid-19, a lethal virus spawned in the ecological mayhem and social squalor on global agribusiness's wild frontier. Thanks to the negligence and cover-ups of the world's rulers, by the time it was called out, in March 2020, it already had a grip. Because of that, the world went into lockdown and was tipped into an economic depression.

Forty million out of work in the United States. Unemployment in Britain set to triple by the end of 2021. A record 30% out of work in South Africa. Hundreds of millions of low-paid workers in the Global South facing a gut-wrenching choice between catching the disease in a crowded sweatshop or street-market and watching their children starve.

The pandemic is still with us. There is, at the time of writing, no clear end in sight. Waves of redundancies and wage cuts are choking demand, driving fresh waves of collapse. Businesses and consumers, facing an uncertain future, are reluctant or unable to spend. A negative 'multiplier effect' is pulling everything down. Some economists are saying the world will take a decade to recover.

A rational world would have organised things differently. We would have shut down the corporate farm complexes, cleared and rebuilt the slums, and made health provision a priority. And now, even in the face of the pandemic, if ordinary people were in control, we would guarantee everyone a job, an income, a home, and basic goods and services.

But we do not live in a rational world: we live in a world of corporate power and competitive capital accumulation powered by the pursuit of profit. It is this dynamic that explains the present crisis of neoliberalism.

The system is afflicted with chronic deflation, a persistent and debilitating lack of demand. This has been exacerbated by neoliberal restructuring of the workforce and work processes, by deregulation and privatisation, by the breaking of union power, which have enabled employers to raise profits and reduce wages. This means 'over-accumulation' of capital and 'under-consumption' by the working class; an economy with productive capacity far in excess of purchasing power; a system overloaded with surplus capital.

Underpinning the crisis are two massive shifts in global capital accumulation. First, during the neoliberal era, the size of the international working class has roughly trebled from 1.2 billion to 3.5 billion, and there has been a seismic shift of world production from the relatively high-wage Global North to the relatively low-wage Global South.

In the sweatshops and factory complexes of slum mega-cities across Asia, Africa, and South America, hundreds of millions of new proletarians experience super-exploitation at the hands of local sub-contractors working for giant transnational corporations; and it is the latter, in control of finance, technology, supply-chains, digitalised information, and markets that cream off the resulting super-profits.

Second, especially but not exclusively in the Global North, there has been a relative shift in the focus of exploitation from the workplace ('the point of production') to the individual household ('the point of consumption and social reproduction'). The spending power of working-class families is hoovered up by mortgages, rents, taxes, utility bills, transport costs, supermarket prices, and, not least, interest on consumer debt.

Debt. That is a matter of special import. We now live in a 'permanent debt economy', where demand is sustained by government, corporate, and consumer debt, and where debt becomes a tradable commodity in its own right, with vast edifices of financial speculation, of casino banking and electronic mega-fortunes, built out of debt-based financial assets.

That is why the system keeps crashing, most spectacularly in 2008, when it was discovered that millions of 'sub-prime mortgages' had been sold to poor people who could not afford to repay them at the height of the speculative boom. That bad debt had been 'diced and spliced' with sound debt and sold on in the form of complex 'financial derivatives', so that the entire world banking system was infected. The only thing that prevented complete meltdown was a series of gargantuan state bailouts to prop up bankrupt private banks.

The state bailouts rebooted the electronic casino. And now, with the real economy in freefall, with incomes shrinking and demand collapsing across the world, we hover on the brink of another financial catastrophe.

Let us now drill down deeper into the inner workings of the system. Neoliberalism's 'economics of the madhouse' threaten the wellbeing of the great majority of humanity and of the ecosystems on which we all depend. To save ourselves and our planet, we have to understand the system, so that we can organise ourselves to overthrow it and replace it with an economy based on democracy, planning, sustainability, and human need.

A history of crisis

Crisis is a normal part of the way capitalism works. But sometimes a crisis is so serious it tips the system into long-term depression, tears society apart, and triggers fascism, war, and even genocide.

There are three kinds of crisis under capitalism – cyclical, structural, and systemic. Cyclical crises typically occur every ten years or so. They happen because capitalism is a system of blind, anarchic, unplanned growth. Every boom ends in a bust.

But the bust, by driving many firms out of business, prepares the ground for a new boom. The effect of the bust is to choke back supply and clear clogged-up markets. The firms that survive can then start a new round of expansion.

Cyclical crises have been compared to the 'breathing' of the system – a recurring pattern of expansion and contraction by which capitalism, in its anarchic way, periodically rebalances supply and demand by bankrupting a swathe of existing capital.

A structural crisis is much more serious and intractable. It is a sustained period of sub-optimal growth when surplus capital builds up inside the system because there are insufficient outlets for profitable investment. The result is protracted stagnation, mass unemployment or underemployment, and austerity cuts.

There have been three or four earlier periods of structural crisis in the history of the system. Some economic historians see the entire period from 1815 to 1848 – when, of course, industrial capitalism was in its infancy – as a sustained period of structural crisis. This was followed by a long boom from 1848 to 1873.

Then the world economy collapsed into what was, unquestionably, a long structural crisis from 1873 to 1896. It was triggered by a financial crash, but what followed was more than two decades when growth rates were barely half what they had been in the preceding period.

This structural crisis – the Long Depression – led to major changes in the way capitalism operated. Smaller firms went to the wall. Big firms became dominant and formed cartels or trusts to fix prices and protect markets. Banks, heavy industry, and the state formed a tight economic alliance, with major firms buoyed up by bank loans and state contracts.

Because home markets were depressed, the imperial powers used their military might to build overseas empires and provide the big firms with new outlets for capital investment.

Because this process was competitive, international tensions rose, an arms race kicked off, and the world finally exploded into war in 1914.

So the structural crisis which began in the 1870s led to a remodelling of capitalism, aggressive imperialism, and, eventually, the industrialised carnage of the First World War, in which 15 million died. That war can be seen as a direct consequence of capitalism's inherent tendency towards over-accumulation, because it was this that drove imperialism and the global struggle for raw materials and markets.

The second great structural crisis was triggered by the Wall Street Crash of 1929. This plunged the world into the Great Depression, with unemployment close to one in three in both Germany and the United States in the early 1930s.

This story is familiar. The Great Depression polarised politics, but fascism triumphed across much of the world and eventually plunged humanity into the Second World War, when 60 million died, the majority of them civilians killed in the genocides implemented by the German Nazis (in Eastern Europe) and the Japanese Militarists (in China). Again, an economic crisis of over-accumulation became a military crisis of imperialist war. A stagnant system led to the horrors of Nanking, Stalingrad, Auschwitz, and Hiroshima.

And again, capitalism was restructured by crisis. A new form of state capitalism emerged. In its most extreme form – Stalinist Russia – the entire national economy was controlled by a party/state bureaucracy. Elsewhere, state infrastructure and arms expenditure meant lucrative contracts for private corporations and provided a basis for economic recovery.

State capitalism underpinned the war economies of 1939-45, and then, after the war, the state-capitalist model became the basis of reconstruction, a new boom, the building of welfare states, and the advent of a 'consumer society'.

The post-war boom – 'the Great Boom' – saw the world capitalist economy grow at a faster rate than at any time in its history. The boom was sustained by US financial power (the dollar became the world's reserve currency), high levels of arms expenditure (during the Cold War), high levels of state expenditure (on infrastructure, housing, schools, hospitals, welfare, etc), and by proactive state intervention to regulate capital and manage demand ('Keynesianism').

This phase in the development of world capitalism came to an end in the early 1970s. Growth rates slowed in the mid to late 60s, and the system then tipped into full-blown crisis in 1973. Two interlocking factors were of decisive significance: the rise of the multinationals; and the squeeze on profits.

As the world economy grew, global markets were increasingly dominated by a relatively small number of corporate giants in each sector. This new stage in what Marx called 'the centralisation and concentration of capital' we discuss in more detail below. What matters here is that nation-state economic management was increasingly incompatible with the power and interests of giant corporations with global reach. Increasingly, state power was trumped by corporate power, with capital able to demand deregulation, lower taxes, subsidies and incentives, etc. in return for investment.

The squeeze on profits was another consequence of the boom. Full employment meant tight labour markets, strong unions, and enhanced bargaining power for organised workers. Higher wages and rising living standards, combined with the increased 'social wage' represented by state spending on housing, education, health, and welfare, meant that the overall distribution of wealth became somewhat more equal: working people got a larger share at the expense of corporate profits and the incomes of the rich and the middle class.

To restore the rate of profit, ruling classes across the world launched a counter-offensive to roll back the popular gains of the post-war period. Social-democratic 'welfare states' in the Global North and 'national-developmental' programmes in the Global South – both involving state intervention, the provision of basic services, and a degree of income redistribution – were dismantled. This is the essential meaning of neoliberalism: it is a 'counter-revolution' by corporate capital at the expense of the working class and the oppressed on a world scale. Let us now explore this in more detail.

The neoliberal counter-revolution

William I Robinson argues that the neoliberal era (from 1975 onwards) has seen a sharp acceleration in the internationalisation of capital and a qualitative shift from merely 'international capital' to 'transnational capital'. The distinction he makes is between 'international' firms that retain a primary national base but move capital and commodities on a global scale, and 'transnational' firms that relocate production itself, with plants in numerous countries, linked together in a web of supply-chains, so that the entire process of capital accumulation becomes fully globalised.

His perspective – developed in a series of seminal books over two decades – offers a holistic view of the world system today. The key observations can be summarised as follows:

- The world capitalist system is afflicted with an intractable crisis of over-accumulation, chronic tendencies to stagnation, and increasingly pathological ways of unloading surplus capital.
- A transnational capitalist class, with associated transnational state apparatuses, has now become the hegemonic fraction of capital on a global scale, dominant over regional, national, and local fractions.
- A globalised process of 'primitive accumulation' has reached its culmination, with virtually the whole of humanity displaced from control over its own means of production and subsumed within global circuits of capital accumulation.
- Capital has now colonised the planet as a whole, is pushing beyond the limits of sustainability, and thus threatens humanity with ecological breakdown and an existential crisis.
- The global working class – now the overwhelming majority of humanity – is divided into a core group in relatively secure jobs, a precarious group in marginal employment, and a surplus group that is effectively excluded, with the former shrinking and the latter two growing rapidly, especially in the context of 'digitalisation' and the 'Fourth Industrial Revolution'.
- Because the global squeeze on working-class incomes means that the working class cannot consume its own product ('under-consumption'), surplus capital ('over-accumulation') is offloaded in increasingly parasitic ways – through financial speculation, debt-driven consumption, pillaging of state assets (privatisation), and 'militarised accumulation'.

Let us consider these forms of accumulation and the way they interlock in more detail. A growing proportion of the wealth of the rich is used to fund financial speculation. In this form of accumulation, nothing is produced, and no socially-useful service provided. Instead, the rich trade financial assets of one sort or another – bonds, shares, mortgages, currencies, etc. These are essentially claims on future value in monetary form. What the rich are actually trading is debt.

The scale of what has been called 'the permanent debt economy' is awesome. In late 2008, the 'value' of the world derivatives market was estimated at $791 trillion. This was *eleven times* the value of the entire world economy. Where the ratio of fictitious capital to real capital is 11:1, you have an unsustainable speculative bubble. Sooner or later, the bubble bursts. When it does, debts cannot be repaid and a tranche of mega-corporations go bankrupt.

Only what happened in 2008 was that the big corporations were bailed out by trillions of dollars of state money. One estimate of US government spending on bailouts between 2008 and 2012 put the total at $30 trillion.

So public money – taxpayer money – our money – was used to prop up private banks and stabilise the global financial system. This meant states becoming heavily indebted. They therefore imposed a decade of austerity that lowered wages, cut pensions and benefits, and eviscerated public services.

The rich, meantime, used the injections of public money to fund a new round of speculation. Total world debt was around $173 trillion (280% of global GDP) at the time of the 2008 crash. It is now around $250 trillion (320% of global GDP). So the world economy is hovering on the brink of another financial collapse.

Oxfam estimated that a few years after the financial crisis, in 2014, the richest 85 billionaires in the world had as much wealth as the poorest half of humanity. Five years after that, in 2019, they estimated that just 26 billionaires had this amount of wealth. The reason for this growing social inequality is simple: the permanent debt economy is a gigantic global mechanism for extracting wealth from working people and siphoning it to the top.

At the base of the great edifice of debt and capital accumulation are ordinary workers and consumers. When you boil it down, the rich accumulate wealth in two main ways.

First, workers are paid less than the value of the work they do, and exploitation at the point of production has increased massively in the neoliberal era. Four processes are at work: a) the breaking of the post-war 'social-democratic consensus' in the Global North so as to redistribute wealth from labour to capital; b) the smashing of national-development plans in the Global South through 'structural adjustment programmes' designed to open up economies to exploitation by transnational capital; c) the relocation of production to the low-wage mega-slums of the Global South; and d) using the 'reserve army of labour' created by a trebling in size of the international working class to undercut the pay, conditions, and bargaining power of workers everywhere.

The consequences are all around us. Even in the Global North, millions of workers are denied permanent, full-time jobs. Millions are on temporary contracts, 'short-hours' contracts, or 'zero-hours' contracts; millions are forced to work part-time or to moonlight; millions are low-paid, insecure, and end up in debt. Even those with decent jobs have faced falling or stagnant wages.

Low pay and high profit are two sides of one equation. The neoliberal counter-revolution of the last 40 years has engineered a huge shift of wealth from workers to bosses.

That is one kind of exploitation. There is another, of increasing importance: exploitation at the point of consumption and social reproduction. This takes three main forms.

The first is payment for the goods and services we need. This involves: the introduction of fees for things that used to be free (like higher education); increased charges for things that used to be subsidised (like transport); routine overpricing of consumer goods by big corporations (which collaborate to fix prices); and the extortionate rents charged by private landlords (in the absence of rent controls).

The second is interest on debt. Household debt has rocketed in the neoliberal era. Mortgage debt, student debt, credit-card debt, pay-day-loan debt, and more have become primary mechanisms by which the corporate rich accumulate wealth.

Debt has risen for three reasons: workers borrow money to compensate for falling wages; bankers encourage borrowing as a source of profit; the system as a whole needs debt to maintain demand in a time of austerity. The effect is to redistribute wealth from bottom to top.

The third mechanism is taxation. Taxes have been cut for the rich and the corporations in the neoliberal era; much of their wealth, in any case, is stashed in tax havens. Working people carry the main burden of state taxes. Some of this is used in socially beneficial ways, like funding education, health, welfare payments, and local services. But much is not.

Tax revenues are used to buy armaments, build detention-centres, fund prestige projects like HS2 and, of course, bail out bankrupt corporations. Even when used in socially beneficial ways, state facilities are privatised, or government contracts are outsourced, so that (our) taxes end up being recycled into (their) profits.

But a fast-rising proportion of this state expenditure is not socially beneficial at all. On the contrary: it is expenditure on what William I Robinson calls 'militarised accumulation' and a 'Global Police State'. We have discussed aspects of this in earlier chapters. Here we focus on the economic aspect. This is how Robinson describes 'militarised accumulation' in his latest book *The Global Police State* (2020):

> ... the global economy is based more and more on the development and deployment of ... systems of warfare, social control, and repression as a means of making profit and continuing to accumulate capital in the face of stagnation – what I term 'militarised accumulation', or 'accumulation by repression'... the ruling groups have acquired a vested interest in war, conflict, and repression as a means of accumulation. As war and state-sponsored violence become increasingly privatised, the interests of a broad array of capitalist groups shift the political, social, and ideological climate towards generating and sustaining social conflict – such as in the Middle East – and in expanding systems of warfare, repression, surveillance, and social control. We are now living in a veritable war economy.

Neoliberalism is a highly parasitic form of capitalism. Much 'economic' activity today is not truly economic at all: nothing is made, nothing is done. Instead there is 'financialised accumulation' – a process whereby wealth is hoovered from consumers in the form of fees, prices, rents, debts, and taxes. Even in the real economy, there is vast expenditure on luxuries for the rich, on armaments and police repression, on advertising and marketing, and on other kinds of waste. And there are devastating consequences – the degradation of Nature, the creation of mega-slums, the spewing out of 'surplus humanity', the mind-crushing boredom of labour for capital, and so much more.

To understand why modern capitalism is so malignant, we must drill down even deeper, to understand the system's long-term dynamics and trajectories.

The centralisation and concentration of capital

Capitalism is the most dynamic form of social organisation in human history. Marx wrote of its 'constant revolutionising of production' and 'uninterrupted disturbance of all social conditions' in The Communist Manifesto of 1848. Twenty years later, in the first volume of Capital, he described that way in which the pursuit of profit powered investment, growth, and rapid increase in the scale of capitalist enterprise.

Take communications. In Marx's day, even in the most developed parts of the world, news moved at the speed of the postal service. Then cables were laid and reports could be transmitted in minutes. But most people still had to wait for a printed newspaper to reach the streets before they caught up. By the time of the Second World War, however, many households had radios. Then, during the 1950s, the TV set became ubiquitous. The internet was invented as recently as 1989, and smartphones took off less than 20 years ago.

And whereas in the mid 19th century, many firms competed in each sector of industry, the pattern today, in the early 21st century, is for a handful of giant corporations to dominate each global market.

The ancient Greek philosopher Heraclitus taught us that all things are in a state of flux and that change is the only constant. This is more apparent today than ever before. What makes capitalism more dynamic than all preceding social systems – what makes it a self-feeding process of exponential growth – is the process of *competitive capital accumulation*.

Unlike earlier forms of competition – like the political rivalry between tribal chieftains, ancient empires, and medieval kingdoms – capital accumulation involves economic competition between rival corporations. Capitalists are compelled to invest in new technologies to avoid being priced out of the market by more efficient competitors using labour-saving machinery. They are subject to the iron law of the market: the need to cut costs, increase output, and reduce prices to stay in business.

The measure of success is profit. The more successful capitalists capture a larger share of the market and make bigger profits. These profits then get reinvested in the business to enhance competitiveness further. The bigger the scale of operations, the more scope there is for investment and innovation. In the long run, this means the bigger firms win out. Small and medium firms with lower margins and less investment capital can often survive in a boom, but are more likely to go bust in a recession.

Marx called this 'the centralisation and concentration of capital' – an inevitable long-term tendency for both ownership to become more centralised and production more concentrated.

It is more obvious now, as we look back. When Marx was writing *Capital*, a plethora of small and medium firms competed with each other. Manchester, the first industrial city, was dominated by the textile industry. There were a hundred or so mills, most under separate owners, the largest employing 2,000 people, most a few hundred or so. By the time of the First World War, however, the largest workplaces were employing tens of thousands – 75,000 at London's Woolwich Arsenal, 70,000 at Essen's Krupp complex in Germany, 40,000 at Petrograd's Putilov works in Russia.

This process – the rise of the giant corporation – has continued to the present. When Walmart, a few years back, was recorded as the world's largest corporation, its annual revenues of half a trillion dollars made it bigger than Greece. In fact, had it been a country, Walmart would have ranked 25th largest in the world, ahead of 157 out of 193 of the countries in the world.

But wait. That was then (2017), and in the three years since no less than four companies have broken the trillion-dollar barrier – Apple, Amazon, Microsoft, and, most recently, Alphabet (Google's parent company).

A similar picture holds for the world economy as a whole. Each major sector is dominated by a small group of transnational corporations. The biggest companies in finance, oil, motors, electronics, communications, pharmaceuticals, private health, armaments, security, and more turn out to be bigger than most countries. We now have a system where the global market in everything from supermarkets to social media is dominated by handfuls of giant conglomerates.

Watching this process of centralisation and concentration for a century, Marxists have adopted the term 'monopoly-capitalism'. Add in recent globalisation and financialisation, and we have 'globalised, financialised monopoly-capitalism' – a bit of a mouthful, but it sums up the key features of the system today in a single phrase.

When there were lots of small and medium firms operating – as in Marx's day – the competition was pretty ruthless. Capitalists hate this: it means risk and the possibility of bankruptcy if you make the wrong call. They crave the certainties of managed markets with guaranteed sales and rising prices. So as soon as they are able, they form cartels or trusts – they create 'oligopolies' where a few firms dominate and manage the market.

Monopoly does not literally mean that one firm controls everything. Typically, each sector is dominated by half a dozen, maybe a dozen, top firms. But these are few enough, and powerful enough, to collaborate, either by formal agreement or tacit understanding, to avoid mutually destructive price competition. The monopolies become 'price-makers' instead of 'price-takers'.

Rising prices are one side of it. Guaranteed sales are the other. The corporations do not just set the price. They also create the 'want'. This becomes increasingly necessary with exponentially rising output of consumer goods. A growing proportion of the stuff churned out is not needed or even desired. So 'demand' has to be actively created through branding, packaging, advertising, redesigns, upgrades, and so on. Consumers are seduced and bamboozled into buying stuff they never knew existed, let alone wanted.

Intrinsic to this is monumental waste. Goods are designed to fall to bits so they have to be replaced. Commodities are denigrated as out-of-date and out-of-fashion within a year. Consumers are bombarded with messages about the need to buy the latest stuff if they want to be cool, sexy, classy, sophisticated.

Needs are not the same as wants. Needs are intrinsic to the human condition – food, clothes, shelter, education, health-care, and more. Wants can be conjured and manipulated by corporate capital to stoke up consumption. Every one of us is subjected to a daily barrage of corporate propaganda, especially nowadays online, with electronic surveillance and data-gathering used increasingly to target marketing at individual consumers through their social-media feeds.

The ideology of the system is 'free market' competition. In fact, markets have never been 'free' in the sense implied in economics textbooks, but they are less free today than ever before. The reality is monopoly-capitalism, managed markets, rip-off prices, artificial wants, and colossal waste.

We are told that consumer 'choice' shapes the market, that 'supply and demand' determine prices. The truth is that monopoly corporations create and control the market.

This brings us to the central contradiction of the economic system. If prices keep going up, the corporations are making profit twice over, once by exploiting their own workers, second time by overcharging consumers. This means ever more profit in the hands of the corporations. At the same time, however, workers/consumers are getting squeezed, reducing overall demand, making it harder to find a market for everything produced.

Consider Walmart again. It pays rock-bottom wages to its two million workers, but it needs high wages everywhere else so consumers can spend in its 12,000 stores. Every capitalist is in the same position. And the bigger the slice taken by profit, the lower the share of workers/consumers – and the wider the gap between what is produced and what can be sold.

This problem – low wages in the factory, high prices in the shops – is inherent in the capitalist system. It operates with an insoluble problem of 'over-accumulation' (of profit) and relative 'under-consumption' (by the working class). But this problem gets much worse under monopoly-capitalism because the corporations are raking in super-profits by managing the market. That is one issue. Here is another. Reduced competition has not only enabled capitalists to accumulate super-profits; it has also undermined their incentive to invest in new production facilities. To build a factory with state-of-the-art robots to compete on a global scale is a massive, long-term, high-risk investment. What if, before the new production comes on-stream, a war, a pandemic, or an economic downturn shrinks the markets and leaves a glut of unsold goods?

Capitalists are risk-averse, especially the corporate bureaucracies that run today's global giants; and the managed markets of monopoly-capitalism make it much easier to avoid risk. So corporations with a cash surplus are nowadays much more likely to invest in government bonds or company shares, buy up privatised state assets, put money into real estate, trade in debt, or speculate on rising asset values.

There has been a massive shift in the neoliberal era from relatively risky long-term productive investment into short-term financial speculation. That shift has been fast-geared by the exceptional mobility of money achieved by modern IT systems. Financialisation offers click-button fixes for capital in search of quick-and-easy profit.

In sum, the centralisation and concentration of capital means a system of monopoly-capitalism. This involves managed markets, super-profits, risk-avoidance, and financial speculation. Capitalism's inherent tendency towards over-accumulation and under-consumption is thereby intensified. The ageing system is afflicted with chronic and endemic stagnation. It has become a zombie economy addicted to debt.

Digitalised dystopia
World capitalism is now set for a sharp intensification of the over-accumulation crisis rooted in the centralisation and concentration of capital. What some are calling a 'Fourth Industrial Revolution' has begun. Hundreds of millions of jobs are imperilled by digitalised automation. On the one hand, capital becomes concentrated and over-accumulated like never before; on the other, vast masses of workers are either displaced into low-paid precarious jobs or jettisoned entirely as 'surplus humanity', thereby, in economic terms, shrinking demand and deepening the crisis of under-consumption.

Consider some basic facts and figures. At peak employment in 1979, General Motors employed nearly 840,000 people and reported earnings of $11 billion. By contrast, in 2012, Google employed just 38,000 people and generated profits of $14 billion.

Nor is it simply a matter of tech companies being low-labour and high-profit. Their products are integral to all modern circuits of capital accumulation and are driving an economic transformation with massive social implications. 'Digitialisation,' argues William I Robinson:

> ... is leading to a new wave of technological development that has brought us to the verge of the 'Fourth Industrial Revolution', based on robotics, 3D printing, the Internet of Things, artificial intelligence (AI) and machine learning, bio- and nano-technology, quantum and cloud computing, new forms of energy storage, and autonomous vehicles. There is now a fusion of technologies across physical, digital, and biological worlds ... While the tech sector that drives forward this new revolution constitutes only a small portion of the gross world product, digitalisation encompasses the entire global economy, from manufacturing and finance to services, and in both the formal and informal sectors. Corporations are now dependent on digital communications and data for all aspects of their business. 'Tech firms,' notes Foulis, 'are becoming the conduit through which people interact with the world. The tech sector becomes a layer that sits across the entire economy.'

The effect on the structure of the global working class will be profound: a massive increase in the proportion of both precarious and surplus. Let us consider two examples. Millions of people expelled from formal employment in recent years have found low-paid precarious work in the gig economy. Uber, for example, has three million drivers working for it worldwide on fake 'self-employed' contracts. In 2016, the company announced plans to replace a million drivers with autonomously driven vehicles. Walmart also has radical plans in relation to the two million workers on its books.   Most are low-paid precarious workers. But Walmart intends introducing robots to carry out inventory and janitorial work in its stores.

Even now, the International Labour Organisation (ILO) reports that 1.5 billion of the world's 3.5 billion workers are in precarious employment. Many of these are recruited from the ranks of the world's 230 million international migrants and 740 million internal migrants. But this immiseration of humanity is set to get much worse. Quite apart from the growing impacts of economic depression, social disruption, armed conflict, and climate change, there will be the impact of the Fourth Industrial Revolution. Robinson again: 'As digitalisation now drives a new round of worldwide restructuring, it promises to extend precariatisation of workers who have employment and also to expand the ranks of surplus humanity excluded from the labour market.'

The Great Depression of the 2020s

Nothing substantive has changed since 2008. The banks are still run like casinos, and the debt mountain is now higher than ever. The neoliberal elite continues to siphon wealth to the top. The corporations continue to grow by driving down wages, privatising public services, devastating natural environments, and propelling us towards climate catastrophe. They are growing the precariat and spewing out the surplus. They are expropriating and despoiling Nature. They are investing in a new industrial revolution that will leave billions destitute.

All this, then coronavirus.

The great liberal economist John Maynard Keynes taught us that economics is not a science. What happens in the economy is the sum of millions of separate decisions, all based on incomplete knowledge and personal quirks, and no-one can second-guess the outcome with confidence.

But we can assume the following: mass redundancies and swingeing wage cuts; deep insecurity and a desire to save not spend; collapsing demand and confidence spreading across the economy; a self-feeding and self-fulfilling depression, as banks, businesses, and consumers assume the worst and rein back.

Far more likely than the 'bounce-back' predicted by some Tories is that we enter what Keynes called 'a permanent underemployment equilibrium' – a new Great Depression.

The bosses are anticipating this. They have already made it clear that millions are going to lose their jobs, and they have started imposing 15% wage cuts on those who remain and tearing up old contracts and agreed terms and conditions.

This is liable to be the beginning of a massive austerity programme, rolling out over years, to reduce costs and sustain profits – an austerity programme that will not only mean mass impoverishment, but will also be self-defeating, in that it will deepen the depression by driving down demand even further.

This new downturn in the world economy will intensify the system's crisis of legitimacy. It will trigger desperation, anger, and resistance. The system will respond by ramping up police repression and peddling racism, nationalism, and militarism.

Neoliberal capitalism – a system of stagnation-slump, permanent debt, parasitic speculation, and grotesque and growing inequality – is the basis of the wealth and power of the international ruling class. They will defend it with utter ruthlessness. They will take us all into an abyss of barbarism if we let them. The rich and their system must be overthrown in the interests of humanity and the ecosystem.

Chapter 8

Can the System Be Reformed?

How do we respond to the crisis? It is inevitable there will be movements of resistance – protests, direct action, strikes, possibly riots. Where people's lives are falling apart, they are driven to radical action.

While socialists are active in all progressive movements of protest and resistance, they aim to organise the working class to take the lead and impose an anti-capitalist solution to the crisis. If the problems flow from the nature of capitalism as a system of exploitation and oppression, then it is the working class – the overwhelming majority of humanity – that must create an alternative to the system.

But it is not so simple. People do not automatically reach revolutionary conclusions in a crisis. Initially, they reach for existing ideas and everyday solutions to fix the problems. This is where politics comes in. People can resort to nationalism, racism, populism, and petty violence if they think it will help. Or they can turn to the left, towards socialist ideas.

But left politics itself is full of contradictions. Mostly this is because of the contradictions that exist within capitalism, within our society, in the economy, inside our heads. Workers appear free – free to move jobs, to move house, to live as they please – but this freedom exists within certain limits, certain rules. A central contradiction of life under capitalism is the nature of wage-slavery, where you have an ideology of human freedom, but in reality the system closes doors to ordinary people on all sides.

The contradictions create confusion. People are encouraged to believe they can 'get on' within the system. The core reality of exploitation and oppression is disguised. Revolutionary conclusions are not automatic; even in a crisis, resistance is not guaranteed, and revolution certainly not.

There already exist mass working-class organisations – trade unions and social-democratic parties – and they are adapted to operate within the system, counterposing the idea of gradual piecemeal change as an alternative to radical change from below. This is the great debate between reform and revolution.

A short history of reformism

Marxists use the term reformism to mean one of two things. Reformism originally started as a strategy for socialism, focusing not on revolutionary action but on getting a legislative majority in parliament and passing a series of laws that would bit by bit create a planned economy. But as the 20th century wound its bloody way through time, reformism abandoned this goal and evolved into a way of simply managing capitalism, not ending it.

These two understandings of reformism exist on a spectrum. They are connected and often exist as a form of political consciousness: politicians and activists might believe they are reforming away capitalism, when in fact they are merely pursuing policies to ameliorate the system. They sing the *Red Flag* at Labour Party Conference, but then support wage restraint across the public sector.

Reformism, then, has evolved from a strategy for achieving socialism through parliament to a modern kind of social-democratic politics that is effectively anti-socialist – anti the radical transformation necessary to achieve a socialist society. The constant conflation of socialism and social-democracy is a damning indictment of the political level of the labour movement. Momentum – the movement inside the Labour Party set up to support the Corbyn leadership – has often exemplified this confusion.

All ideas are embedded in the real lives of human-beings, and evolve as people struggle to shape the world around them. The idea of socialism goes back to the American and French Revolutions in the late 18th century. It arose from the failure of these 'bourgeois' republican revolutions to deliver on their promise of general emancipation. When the French 'Third Estate' (the commoners) took power in 1789, a sharp split between the propertied elite and the mass of ordinary people emerged. Out of the 'Fourth Estate' came the idea of a more far-reaching social revolution.

This idea bore fruit in Britain in 1838 with the launch of the Chartists, the first mass working-class movement in history. The Chartists united around demands for six reforms to parliament that would break the stranglehold of the old aristocrats and the emerging bourgeoisie and empower working men (but not women) to vote. But while they agreed on the demands, they disagreed fundamentally on how to achieve them. The movement was split between a 'moral force' wing that sought to persuade and a 'physical force' wing that believed those in power would not willingly surrender their position and that things could be changed only by armed struggle.

In the end, all but one of the reforms was passed (the demand for annual parliaments remains unrealised), but there was no revolution. Does this prove that reformist strategies work?

The power of the Chartist movement was rooted in the threat of militant action. Chartist groups up and down the country armed themselves and drilled in the use of weapons. Uprisings by Chartists in Newport (1839) and Halifax (1842) as well as a massive demonstration in Kennington Park in London in 1848 terrified the authorities. This threat, and further militant action in subsequent decades, forced a steady succession of concessions – democratic reforms – over the next century.

Note that the working class had to threaten to overthrow the bourgeoisie to realise its claim to greater political liberty; it had to threaten revolution to win reform – the democratisation of parliament. Nonetheless, this led Marx and many of his followers to the conclusion that socialism might be achieved in a country like Britain through parliamentary action; that it might be possible to win an electoral majority for the overthrow of capitalism on the basis of working-class votes; and for this to be implemented by a radical government using the existing state apparatus.

Marx died before the new trade unions combined with emerging socialist groups to create mass social-democratic parties, and long before any of these parties came to wield governmental power. He therefore did not live to see how electoralism changes the nature of left politics, how it shifts first the tone, then the tempo, and ultimately the direction of the socialist movement.

Towards the end of the 19th century, Marxists across Europe built mass working-class parties, calling them either socialist or social-democratic. They formed them into a 'Second International' (following the First International in which Marx and Engels had been involved). These parties built trade unions, sometimes in illegal conditions, in Germany, Russia, and elsewhere. They advocated class war, the socialisation of the economy under workers control, and (at times) revolutionary politics.

In Britain, however, the Marxists were a much weaker force. Instead, it was the trade unions that launched the Labour Party. Marxists at the founding of the Labour Representation Committee in 1900 put a proposal for the Labour Party to be based on class struggle and socialism, but Keir Hardie and the union leaders opposed this; the new party was to be the political arm of union functionaries.

The emergence of mass trade unions in the 1880s had been crucial for the developing working class, allowing it to organise in the workplaces both to defend itself against the bosses and to formulate wider demands for improved living conditions. The slogans raised – like 'a fair day's pay for a fair day's work' – give an indication of the political basis of trade unionism: it was about 'fair pay' under capitalism. This is typical of the fog of reformism. 'Fair pay' is impossible under capitalism, for the source of profit is the exploitation of labour; if workers were paid the full value of their work, there would be no profit.

Reformism as an ideology – the view that there is a parliamentary route to socialism and that by winning elections socialists can implement laws to socialise the economy – emerged in Britain and Germany at the turn of the 20th century.

In Britain, parliamentary politics was in the DNA of the Labour Party from day one. But in Germany, the route to reformism was more gradual and theoretical. The German Social Democratic Party was initially revolutionary, but its day-to-day work involved a struggle for reforms. Germany was a fast-industrialising and emerging imperialist power able to afford reforms for workers – higher wages, welfare legislation, and so on.

The German SDP ended up building 'a state within a state', a network of reading groups, cycling clubs, leisure centres, educational facilities, and much more. Here was the main focus of the SPD: making life more liveable for workers *within* the system. The intellectuals of the SPD began to theorise the politics they practised, leading to a spectacular row in the party between the revolutionaries, led by Rosa Luxemburg, and the 'revisionists', led by Edward Bernstein.

Likewise, in Britain, the richest country in the world at the time, trade unions and Liberal politicians delivered some reforms for workers. In fact, the Labour Party only really began to grow when the Liberals reneged on their promises and Labour became the main advocate of gradual reform.

If you read the journals and newspapers of Social Democratic and Labour parties of this time, they are full of radical-sounding talk, of calls for a crusade for socialism, of a life-and-death struggle against capitalist tyranny. But this was only talk. The key to understanding reformism is always to look at what they do, not what they say.

The leaders of these parties had decided to pursue a path of gradual change, not revolutionary struggle. Many sincerely believed that this was the true road to socialism. The difference between gradualists and revolutionaries seemed minor, theoretical, an abstract argument – until the First World War.

Then, in the crisis of 1914, the European workers movement was irrevocably split over whether to oppose or support the war. The Second International (of socialist parties) fell apart. Despite only a few years earlier having solemnly sworn to use any means necessary to prevent an imperialist war, most parties ended up beating the drums of war in the interests of their respective capitalist classes. The result was 15 million dead, the vast majority of them ordinary working people.

In most socialist parties, only a minority opposed the war on internationalist grounds when it began; many of these ended up in prison. In Russia, however, the dominant Bolshevik wing of the RSDLP (Russian Social-Democratic Labour Party) opposed the war, agitated for revolution, and eventually organised the overthrow of a pro-war Provisional Government in Russia in the October Revolution of 1917.

This took Russia out of the war and triggered a wave of revolution from below that spread across Europe and eventually brought the war as a whole to an end. The German Revolution in 1918 ended Germany's involvement in the war. But the German Social Democratic leaders – elevated to power by that revolution – then used violent right-wing militias to suppress the workers movement. Revolutionaries such as Rosa Luxemburg were murdered to preserve German capitalism.

This was an important lesson: it showed that at the moment of revolution, reformism is not merely a different route to the same goal; it is an integral part of the existing social order and can become an actively counter-revolutionary force willing to smash popular movements to defend the system in a crisis.

The theory and practice of reformism
The initial aim of reformist socialism was simple: to use the existing state machinery – parliament, elections, the judiciary, the civil service, local government – to implement socialism. It was based on the view that the state is relatively neutral, and that just as the capitalist class uses its machinery to pursue its political agenda, so too might the working class. It was really a question of arithmetic: how many workers' representatives could you get elected to the legislature?

The socialist MPs would propose laws to nationalise the economy, to create workers' co-operatives, to democratise the running of public services, and they would simply out-vote the Tories, Liberals, and others. Then the civil service and local government would loyally implement the new laws, because that is how democracy works, and if there was any unlawful opposition to the new laws, the police would be there to suppress it.

Reformists imagine the state to be like a car. If the bosses are driving, it goes in the wrong direction. If socialists take the wheel, they can turn it around.

But the state is not like a car. It is an administrative and repressive apparatus staffed by members of the ruling class and their loyalist functionaries. It is deeply embedded within the existing social order, and is suffused with its values, protocols, and procedures. It is an instrument of capitalist class rule, not a neutral device to be repurposed to achieve its overthrow.

The contradiction embedded within mass working-class organisations is between the actuality of the class war and the political compromise of the leaders of those organisations. The working class has no interest in capitalism and will continue to be exploited and oppressed so long as the system survives. But most workers live their lives simply trying to get by; few draw revolutionary conclusions from their experiences of class society; often enough they do not even think of such experiences – wage cuts, rotten contracts, bullying supervisors, hospital waiting lists, underfunded schools, racist police, rip-off landlords, and so much more – in class terms at all. If their boss sacks them, they look for a new job. If they cannot pay the rent, they look for somewhere cheaper. If times are hard and 'everyone' needs to tighten their belts – it never *is* everyone – people grudgingly go along with it. If the government says austerity is necessary because of too much debt, people assume it must be so. They grumble and complain, but they see these things as part of normal life. What can one do? Some workers join trade unions to get protection at work, but the unions themselves are reformist organisations: they negotiate a modest wage increase or slightly improved terms and conditions; but they do not seek to end the capital-wage relationship itself.

This contradiction – between the interests of the working class and the conservatism of working-class organisation – is also evident in the social role of the bureaucrats and functionaries of both unions and social-democratic parties. The officials are often relatively well paid, have a great deal of influence, and form a bureaucratic caste shielded from criticism by members. Reformism is not just an 'idea'; it has a material basis in the worldview and interests of this stratum of people.

Because reformist ideology is focused on passing laws in favour of the working class, it is inseparable from the electoral and parliamentary systems of the various capitalist states. This leads to both electoral fetishism (obsessing over whether policies will be popular with voters) and nationalism (because the nation-state becomes the centre of political action). This reduces internationalism to tokenistic slogans or appeals for solidarity; only the electoral/parliamentary struggle on the national terrain really matters.

A party like Labour suffers from what Ralph Miliband termed 'parliamentary cretinism' – a dogmatic fixation on parliament as the sole institution of genuine power in the country. Getting more MPs elected on a slightly more left-wing basis is the *raison d'être* of the Labour Party, including the Labour Left (and, at a local level, getting more councillors elected). This parliamentary fixation explains why MPs have always enjoyed a wide measure of political independence from their party: they are required to play by the rules of a political system rooted in the capitalist state and quite alien to the traditions of working-class democracy.

Their parliamentary fetishism involves reformist parties in following strictly constitutional methods. The law in a capitalist state can be a powerful weapon for use against the working class; anti-union laws are an obvious example. This means workers must break the law to wage effective class struggle – 'when injustice becomes law, defiance becomes duty' – but the Labour Party regards law-breaking as anathema. Since MPs use parliament to enact reforms, they feel obliged to respect the legislative process, even when they oppose the laws being passed. This can lead to situations where Labour actively opposes mass movements of resistance.

Reformism in crisis

Until the 1980s, there had been decades of economic growth in the advanced capitalist countries from which many workers benefitted. Increasing productivity led to higher wages and Keynesian state intervention helped soften the worst excesses of free-market capitalism. But from the 1980s onwards, capitalist classes across the world, led by Britain and the USA, shifted policy and unleashed all-out class war against trade unions, the working class, and the oppressed.

The scope for reforms was thereafter severely curtailed. The old social-democratic consensus was broken, replaced by neoliberalism, corporate power, and the enrichment of the 1%. In Britain, Labour has not won a national election on a social-democratic platform since 1974. Its three victories in 1997, 2001, and 2005 were under the leadership of Tony Blair, a neoliberal supporter of privatisation (and imperialist war) opposed to his own party's social-democratic tradition; Labour under Blair was a party of 'counter-reforms'.

Across Europe, social-democratic parties have faced declining membership, low poll ratings, and being locked out of power for decades. Many social-democratic parties embraced globalisation and neoliberalism in the 1990s and ended up attacking their own working-class base, demoralising their supporters, and driving increasing numbers to the right – even towards nationalism and fascism.

Socialist strategy starts from the belief that the working class can (and must) organise to fight the bosses, the landlords, and the state that backs them, and from the belief that this elemental class struggle can evolve into a struggle against the system as a whole, with the possibility of the overthrow of the capitalist class and the establishment of a new system based on revolutionary democracy from below.

Reformists, on the other hand, propose waiting for the next general election and the chance to win a majority of reform-minded MPs. Rather than socialism being based on the self-activity of workers in the pursuit of their own interests, it is about electing politicians to do things for us.

Reformist social-democrats like to project an image of themselves as practical, as 'serious' about politics. They are not shouty, placard-waving protestors, but people engaged in the real business of winning elections and gaining power. But the reformist, parliamentary route to socialism is far from practical; in fact, it turns out to be utterly utopian, for the following reasons:

a) It assumes that the state is neutral, when it is not.
b) It assumes that the capitalist class will surrender power peacefully, when it will not.
c) It assumes that the drip-drip of quantitative change will eventually lead to social transformation, which it will not.
d) It assumes that class oppression can be eliminated by legislation and regulation from on high, which it cannot.

Labour under Corbyn appeared to represent a partial break with this tradition of social-democratic reformism, of parliamentary socialism, but the break seemed radical only because of the legacy of Blairism; it was, in fact, merely a return to the more overtly reformist tradition of the 1970s and 1980s.

Some of the Labour front bench were to be seen on picket lines, but the party remained wedded to its electoral/parliamentary strategy. There was some hope at the beginning that Momentum might act as an organiser of political protests and class resistance, but that idea was rapidly dropped and it became little more than a top-down platform for waging a faction fight inside the party.

This fixation on internal politics and electoral prospects meant that Labour – even when run by the Left – did nothing to build trade unions, to promote active solidarity, to support resistance to job losses, low pay, high rents, and so on.

Reformism has failed: revolution is necessary
Reformism has been highly successful in winning the support of working people because it appears to conform to a living reality. For many, life seems to get better over time. You start off working in low-paid jobs, but you work your way up. You rent a small flat when you are young, but eventually you get to buy somewhere of your own. Most manage to get by, and many see things improve as they get older. And in this context, in so far as change is necessary, the easiest way to get it looks like being through elections and parliament. We usually leave such things to professional politicians while we get on with our lives. This is the foundation for mass reformism as a political current.

But there are moments in history when the system breaks down, society is torn apart, and people's lives fall to bits. Then it is no longer a matter of simply getting by; it becomes a matter of survival. Trade unions struggle to provide basic protection – of jobs, wages, and terms and conditions. And social democracy discovers that the space for reform shrinks to nothing as the system demands austerity and repression.

Millions can be radicalised in a systemic crisis; millions can be driven to take militant action because they have become desperate for a way out. Then there is a need for revolutionary organisation to capture the moment: to canalise the discontent, fan the flames, and turn mass social despair into an active revolutionary force.

This does not mean a sudden end to reformism. Many will retain illusions in parliamentary socialism. Many will cling to the idea that the Left can regain control of the Labour Party, win a general election on a radical platform, and legislate for a socialist transformation. Revolutionaries do not believe that this is possible; but they must work alongside those who retain such illusions. What matters is unity in the struggle to defend the interests of the working class and the oppressed, and unity in the struggle to change the world; and that struggle will provide us all with a sure test of alternative strategies for socialism.

But our view is clear: the whole history of 120 years of Labour reformism has shown its grave limitations; and now we face what is perhaps the greatest crisis of all, when revolutionary solutions seem more imperative than ever before. Labour under Starmer is hopelessly incapable of responding effectively to the scale of the crisis now unfolding – a systemic and compound crisis, with ecological, economic, social, and political dimensions, that poses an existential threat to the whole of humanity. Reformism is limited at the best of times; it is quite useless in the face of climate catastrophe, societal breakdown, and surging fascism.

Chapter 9

The Working Class and the Oppressed

Labour cannot emancipate itself in the white skin where in the black it is branded.
Marx

The Social-Democrat's ideal should not be the trade-union secretary, but the tribune of the people, who is able to react to every manifestation of tyranny and oppression, no matter where it appears, no matter what stratum or class of the people it affects; who is able to generalise all these manifestations and produce a single picture of police violence and capitalist exploitation; who is able to take advantage of every event, however small, in order to set forth before all his socialist convictions and his democratic demands, in order to clarify for all and everyone the world-historic significance of the struggle for the emancipation of the proletariat.
Lenin

There has never been a better time to revisit the question of oppression, that most protean of antagonists and capitalism's henchman. Oppression brings together two distinct elements that differentiate it from similar, related phenomena (bigotry) and related human cognitive errors (prejudice). It involves systemic prejudice, which is directed at a group of people for some perceived or actual characteristic that they share.

While oppressions have both material and historical foundations, they are treated as though they are 'natural' occurrences that exist outside the specific dynamics of any particular class society. Understanding that this is not the case is crucial to understanding the role oppressions play.

A quick gazetteer of oppression

Jingoism is aimed at people from 'othered' nationalities, often stemming from the nationalist and militarist myth-making that were fundamental to the 19th century construction of nation-states. Eric Hobsbawm's work documents this at length.

Racism is directed at those whose 'phenotypical' form (an organism's observable traits) or perceived lineages place them in a group that has been historically 'othered', often with complex roots in nationalism, slavery, hyper-exploitation, colonialism/imperialism, and religious sectarianism. Racism often overlaps with, but cannot be conflated to, jingoism.

Religious sectarianism and oppression also have overlaps with racism (as in the case of Islamophobia and antisemitism) and nationalism (as in the contemporary cases of the also-racist persecution of Palestinians, Rohingya, Uighur, Roma, Gypsies and Travellers, and many others).

Disabilism targets an umbrella of people who are impacted (sometimes visibly, sometimes invisibly) by disabling social relations. Such people might have physical impairments, mental health conditions, chronic illnesses, or even be 'neurodivergent' (i.e. have a variation in their brains that makes their mental functions different from the norm). A society that is not focussed on enabling human flourishing, like capitalism, will tend to treat disabled people (especially from the working class) as if they are merely burdens.

Like disabilism, ageism is directed at the young and old because class society in general, and in this instance capitalist class society, sees them as drains on resources. Such repulsive and anti-human conceptions of what are just the usual cycles of human maturation find their ultimate expression in fascistic cults of youth, notably in Fascist Italy, Nazi Germany, and Militarist Japan in the 1930s.

Misogyny is the hatred of women and the primary tool of the patriarchy (the rule of men). Women have been socially marginalised in class society owing to the dehumanising ways such a society treats human reproduction and the division of labour. This is related to women's allocation to 'shadow work' (unpaid labour), which is largely domestic work in and around the home.

Women's oppression is rooted in bourgeois conceptions of the family. Despite radical changes, the family – and the misogyny and assumptions about a 'woman's place' to which it gives rise – remains central to capitalist society. The family means: low-cost maintenance, reproduction, and socialisation of the labour force; high levels of privatised household consumption (and therefore demand for goods and services); and a primary mechanism of social control, where conformity and obedience to authority can be inculcated.

Homophobia, which impacts men who are attracted to men and women who are attracted to women, and biphobia, which is directed at those attracted to both sexes, is also rooted in the ideology of the family. Transphobia is directed at those whose gender identity does not align with what was assigned to them at birth, which encompasses both binary (women and men) and non-binary people.

Oppression directed against LGBTIQ+ (lesbian, gay, bisexual, transgender, intersex, questioning, asexual) people has a complex relationship to misogyny, since people whose sexuality or gender identity is different from that required in the social reproduction of class society threaten core assumptions of that society.

This is not, and cannot be, comprehensive. Oppression emerges from material factors (the enslavement of Black people, the debasement of women to mere reproduction, the threat bisexual people pose to the family unit as narrowly conceived by bourgeois society), but this is mediated by regionally diverse cultures, which are not mechanistically determined by economy.

The fact is, oppression latches onto many facets of life and society, and is never static. That is why, when we see decreases in sexist attitudes in some areas of social life, for example, we can simultaneously see increases in racism and classism, or vice versa. And although almost all oppressions within class society share substrates, it is not always the case that they necessarily speak to each other.

Oppression and capitalism

If oppression is not natural, why does it seem to be the case that we cannot live in a society without it? Why, even when things are good, is there always some new group being pitched as the 'reason' for society's ills, the objects against whom others can freely punch down.

Prejudice might well be an inviolable facet of human cognition. We tend to abstractly categorise things, people, and ideas, and then to mistake – 'reify' – those categories for actual things, people, and ideas. But oppression is different because it is systemic.

Young children will frequently form prejudices against one another on the flimsiest pretexts (freckles, glasses, bigger than usual ears), which just as frequently vanish as whimsically as they were conceived. What is interesting is why some prejudices (allowing that prejudice itself can be limitlessly arbitrary) gain a strong purchase on the collective social imagination.

The key point here is that oppression plays a critical part in the maintenance of capitalist reproduction. Here, it is important to distinguish oppression within capitalist society from its close counterpart, exploitation. Exploitation applies to all workers. They have to sell their labour-power to earn a living; they trade their labour-power out of necessity in the market-place.

Most of the oppressed are exploited (i.e. they are working class). Precisely because they are marginalised and discriminated against, they are even less likely to become part of the ruling class or the middle class than other people born into the working class. They therefore bear a double burden: exploited *and* oppressed.

The oppressed serve as a buffer. They distract the rest of society from its own suffering. They allow other workers to become invested in the maintenance of their own invisible chains. This scapegoat role is a shifting one, the focus moving periodically from one oppressed group to another.

In Britain, we have seen this emphasis jump like an infection, from Black people and Asians, to gay people, to people of Muslim faith, to the disabled, to Eastern Europeans, to Travellers, to migrants, to transgender people, and back again, most times encompassing all of these groups simultaneously but in varying degrees of intensity.

Covid-19 and other illuminations of racism

In late April 2020, nearly a month after Britain locked down due to the coronavirus pandemic, a curious phenomenon became observable; namely the majority of the doctors and nurses dying from the pandemic were from a Black, Asian, and Minority Ethnic, or 'BAME', background. Could this have been mere coincidence, despite the fact that BAME people made up only 20% of the NHS staff?

Many media outlets and government outfits seemed to think so, as they scratched their heads, arriving at every kind of explanation and excuse – from Vitamin D deficiency to behavioural tendencies. Few were willing to address the elephant in the room – systemic discrimination and structural inequalities.

As those formerly deemed unskilled and undesirable are rebranded 'key workers', there was an apparent over-representation of BAME workers within this group. Uber, bus, and delivery drivers; cleaners, orderlies, and nurses; security guards; post workers; shop assistants; and many others who worked in precarious occupations, but faced heightened exposure to the virus due to the customer-facing nature of their work. The concentration of BAME people in these roles is not an accident, but an artefact of a sustained reproduction of hyper-exploited labour, through legacies of colonialism, slavery, and institutional racism in the US, Britain, and many other places.

When the Windrush generation – at the time of writing still being deported from Britain – first arrived, there were sanctioned jobs they were expected to do, to help the country 'get back on its feet' in the post-war years. These low-paying service jobs were the approved roles for Black people. The underlying assumptions are still with us.

Edward Enninful, the first Black editor of *Vogue Magazine*, was racially profiled in his place of work, when a security guard in the building denied him entry and referred him to the service door. As appalling as such set-ups are anyway (that we employ 'poor doors' in the 21st century), Enninful's encounter is all too familiar. This sort of informal racialised policing has a harmful psychological impact on people of colour, and when adopted as a government policy, as seen with the Windrush scandal and the UK's 'hostile environment', they can have devastating consequences.

When this becomes a *formal* policing strategy, the results are deadlier. A Black man walking into a shop is already deemed suspect; he is examined with closer attention, and any misstep can result in a fatal outcome. This was the case with George Floyd, where a bounced cheque at a supermarket cost him his life, as he was publicly lynched in broad daylight by police officer Derek Chauvin.

Or take the case of Paulette Wilson. A Black woman who had spent 40 years working in Britain, she was hoping for peaceful retirement when hurled into a bureaucratic hell, including incarceration in a detention-centre, because her records had been destroyed by the Home Office and she had fallen victim to the 'hostile environment' state racism of the Tory Government. Her reward was an untimely death at the age of 64, with no compensation for her abusive treatment.

BAME people (as well as other members of the oppressed) often traverse the world with an extra layer of caution, conscious that their identity may be weaponised against them at any time. The knock-on impact of this is a further diminution of control over their own fate, and a reduced capacity to fight the multiple exploitations and oppressions they face, from above and below. The cycle of poverty is therefore reproduced, with BAME people concentrated in poorer areas, with fewer opportunities, and in effect, exposed to the many ravages that cycle through society, be it a virus or economic collapse.

Oppression and identity

Capitalism uses permutations and multitudes of oppressed people to secure its reproduction through time. So why is it that these groups do not often band together – with each other and with the exploited as a whole – so as to transcend the boundaries imposed upon them, unite the forces of resistance, and push back against the system?

Occasionally they do, and these are the groundswells of solidarity and progressive advance we witness throughout history. But they are occasional precisely because, insofar as capitalism remains intact, they eventually get knocked back and dissipated, often through violent repression.

The American Civil Rights Movement of the 1960s was one such example, where we saw solidarity across racial lines, as Black-led fights for equality and freedom from oppression were joined by White allies, pushing towards the same aim.

The result? In 1969 Fred Hampton, a revolutionary leader and member of the Black Panther Party (BPP), was working on developing closer ties between the BPP and other groups, when a 14-man FBI assassination team murdered him during a pre-dawn raid. He was one of many such leaders to be brutally slain by the Federal government during this period. Critically acclaimed author Jay Feldman has written extensively on how the FBI worked knowingly to divide white and Black workers and destroy the revolutionary potential of the Civil Rights Movement.

Earlier this year in May, a similar group of diverse peoples took to the streets of America and Britain, making the same demands for 'Black Lives', as their foremothers and forefathers had done nearly six decades earlier.

During the Thatcher years, a group of LGBTIQ+ people joined forces to support striking miners, raising money to support miners' families during the bitter year-long struggle against pit closures in 1984-5; and this was reciprocated when the National Union of Mineworkers came out in support of LGBTIQ+ rights and led the 1985 London Pride Parade – an event later immortalised in the 2014 film *Pride*.

Gay rights have progressed further since the turn of the century, yet, today, transgender people are fighting for recognition and the self-same rights thought to have been won decades ago. So what has happened? How did we end up here again?

The answer is not straightforward. And it is not that people from different oppressed groups cannot see their plight in other groups' struggles, or that the allies of one oppressed group cannot recognise equivalences across the different struggles. But it is in the interest of the ruling class and corporate capital to see these groups divided – and therefore easier to control.

Within the power structures of the system, privileges, however tenuous, are apportioned to different groups, even among the oppressed. This gives some an interest, however marginal, in defending privileges – and thereby acting as agents for the oppressor. We see different oppressed groups holding onto their chains as they try to preserve their place within capitalist power structures. And so it was in America that White indentured workers who once saw their fate mirrored in that of the enslaved Africans toiling in the fields were granted the gift of 'Whiteness' – so as to prevent these groups, who together far outnumbered their oppressors, from banding together to fight for general emancipation.

The newly minted group of 'Whites' (which at the time excluded the Italians and the Irish) were told that they were 'better' than – racially superior to – Africans, who were labelled 'Negroes', 'Blacks', or 'Niggers'. This extra leverage of Whiteness, which involved only marginal benefits for most, often meant, and often still means, that the most adamantly racist and determined defenders of 'white supremacism' are the poorest of workers – those who stand to gain most from working with their Black counterparts to overturn their oppression

This pattern is replicated across time and space, drawing more groups of people into the realm of the oppressed, as they become surplus to capital's requirements. The Keynesian economist Joan Robinson noted: 'The misery of being exploited by capitalists is nothing compared to the misery of not being exploited at all.' This, of course, is true only in class society; but the point is crucial, for the divisions between the securely employed, the precariously employed, and the unemployed underpin the whole edifice of oppression in capitalist society.

What is happening when we see previous gains by the oppressed reversed, and earlier movements stymied, is that capital is reasserting itself. This divide-and-conquer strategy is a bedrock of class society.

The targeting of oppressed groups is never simply random. It tends to be those whose presence and activity is deemed most threatening to capitalist interests, either because they are surplus to requirements, or because they threaten the structures of capitalist reproduction. Unemployed Black youth – 'surplus humanity' in capitalist terms – are routinely demonised because they are perceived to be a potentially militant threat to the social order. Feminists and LGBTIQ+ activists threaten the patriarchal family. Roma and Travellers are attacked because their nomadic way of life does not conform to the imperatives of capital accumulation. Muslims become an 'enemy within' in the context of imperialist wars in the Middle East. And so on.

The discourse of oppression is developed after the fact, but the aim is always the preservation of capitalism, where exploiters are able to carry on with the business of profiteering, using marginalised groups as scapegoats for social failures. In this way, as long as the system endures, we keep ending up back in the same position.

Processes, unity, and contradiction

The Left has too often made mistakes about oppression and exploitation. The basis of these mistakes is to reify identity or class, that is, to treat a category (an idea, an abstraction) as a thing. Class reductionists treat class in this way: that is, they regard people who once belonged to the working class as still part of it even when their social position and therefore their loyalties have changed, while others are not accepted as working class even when they are trade unionists fighting exploitation. They do so because the abstraction becomes more real than class as it actually exists. The point is not just that class has changed – as liberals love to argue – but that class is not a static category, but a dynamic process.

This is also true of the categories of the oppressed, albeit with differences. So Blackness emerges when *both* racial pseudoscience 'justifies' certain anti-Black practices (such as transatlantic slavery or European colonialism) *and* Black people realise a historical agency in solidarity and opposition to such practices (in anti-racism, anti-colonialism). Likewise, LGBTIQ+ identities emerge out of *both* homophobia, transphobia, etc and the coalescence of identities in resisting this oppression. Harmful fragmentations arise from seeing identities not as a *process*, but as transhistorical, static, timeless, 'natural' rather than as social categories. This results in separatisms, exclusionary politics, an unwillingness to recognise new oppressions as they emerge, or acknowledge either advances or erosions of gains.

Similarly, class reductionism treats class not as what emerges when workers unite to challenge their exploitation, or abolish exploitation by creating a new, classless society, but as a timeless quality adhering to special people (identified by things as flimsy as regional accents, particular vocations, etc). They then accuse the oppressed of fragmenting the struggle of the exploited by focusing on their oppression. Such a false theory of class means that oppressed people can feel excluded from movements that should embrace them.

Marxism, class, and oppression

For socialism to be achieved it must be, in Marx's conception, the self-emancipation of workers. Atomised workers in competition with each other cannot emancipate themselves. Only workers who unite as a class and fight collectively can change the world.

Marx also argued that the working-class movement has to fight every form of oppression, for its purpose and effect is to divide and weaken the workers' struggle. Lenin put it very succinctly when he said that a socialist activist is not first and foremost a trade unionist, but a 'tribune of the oppressed'.

The unity of the exploited and the oppressed in the struggle for social emancipation is the aim: that is the only way to create a political force powerful enough to overthrow the state, dispossess the rich, and create the basis for the construction of a new democratic society.

How do these broad generalisations relate to theories of oppression and 'intersectionality'?

The metaphor of 'intersections' of oppression, conceived as an attempt to capture (not reify) the multi-layered and overlapping character of oppression, was first conceived by civil rights lawyer and Black feminist philosopher Kimberlé Williams Crenshaw:

> Consider an analogy to traffic in an intersection, coming and going in all four directions. Discrimination, like traffic through an intersection, may flow in one direction, and it may flow in another. If an accident happens in an intersection, it can be caused by cars travelling from any number of directions and, sometimes, from all of them. Similarly, if a Black woman is harmed because she is in the intersection, her injury could result from sex discrimination or race discrimination.

Intersectionality theory has, however, sometimes been reified in the context of postmodernism and neoliberalism. Postmodernism – a portmanteau of related theories centred on the basic idea that no single overarching 'grand narrative' is capable of explaining the world as a whole – has encouraged a multiplication of 'discourses' and 'identities' as a means towards self-valuation, self-assertion, and self-empowerment.

But has it delivered? Postmodernism has a rotten reactionary core: the idea that human beings cannot arrive at a common understanding of the world as it really is, on the basis of which they might organise themselves collectively to change it. Instead of promoting the unity necessary to take on the power of capital and the state, postmodernism celebrates abstracted ideas of 'difference' and 'diversity'. You and I can choose an 'identity', but the rich continue to rule because united historical struggle against oppression and exploitation is foreclosed.

In addressing identity politics and intersectionality, the theorist Asad Haider has tried to place Crenshaw's work in its context:

> She cited cases in which courts determined that an anti-discrimination lawsuit 'must be examined to see if it states a cause of action for race discrimination, sex discrimination, or alternatively either, but not a combination of both'. She went on to link this specific legal question to the general problem already described by the Combahee River Collective: that single-issue political frameworks would end up centring the most privileged members of a group, marginalising those whose identities exposed them to other forms of subordination.

Haider argues that intersectionality is subverted when its invocation forgets that it was intended to critique official denials that many people experience multiple oppressions: this is what matters. Postmodernist interpretations of intersectionality have, in fact, hollowed out its radical content. As the work of Tommy J Curry has shown, this can even cause the oppression of some groups to be partially erased. Black men are seen as empowered by maleness, rather than oppressed as Black men, and this has meant that 'the Black male has been the most ignored subject in the attempt to pluralise identities intersectionally'.

Oppression is at the core of Marxism. The working class will never liberate itself while divided against itself. Any self-described socialist, anarchist, or Marxist who subordinates oppression to class understands neither. While electoral coalitions frequently necessitate giving ground to reactionaries on issues such as immigration law, revolutionary struggle to abolish class society is only – and often irreparably – weakened by such concessions.

Marx was famously anti-utopian, but by this he meant he was opposed to any form of socialist organisation or doctrine that imposed blueprints from above on the working class. While Marx was circumspect, then, in speculating about a future society, there are many indications scattered throughout his work of what such a society might look like.

The abolition of oppression opens up a range of possibilities that are truly exciting; every human relationship today, between women and men, Black and White, gay and straight, trans and cis, is filtered through distorting social relations that are 'naturalised' by ideology. As Marx wrote, 'The ideas of the ruling class are in every epoch the ruling ideas.'

To put it bluntly, under class society the quality of our relationships is diminished; this spiritual violence impacts every human being of every class, albeit in different ways. It reduces and diminishes what it is to be human, so that we can only begin to scratch the surface of the shared possibilities of humanity. There are many reasons to seek to overcome capitalism, not least the impending climate crisis that threatens our species survival, but to imagine the cosmic joke of a species with such potential never managing to seize control of its own destiny and create a society fit for its full capacities is perhaps the greatest reason of all.

Nor is this goal a merely distant one: in working together now, as comrades, we can change ourselves and each other – that, indeed, is why Marxism is rooted in struggle as a self-transforming activity. Solidarity – among all the exploited and oppressed, the great majority of the human race – is not an abstraction. It involves real relations between real human beings, and offers some of the greatest opportunities for our own personal and collective advancement within the limits of our current society – as well as providing the essential means finally to end 5,000 years of exploitation and oppression in class society.

Chapter 10

From Anti-Capitalist Resistance to Post-Capitalist Transformation

Neoliberalism has been the dominant mode of capitalist rule for 40 years. The history of this period, especially since 2000, has shown repeatedly that the present political domination of the Far Right at government level was not inevitable.

On the contrary, the social system in which finance-capital is dominant, employment insecure, inequality massive, and racist and sexist ideologies running riot, all this is the product of conscious choices and the ideological/political struggle of right-wing governments, parties, and think-tanks.

Neoliberalism was made by people, and can be undone by other people. Capitalism itself was made by people – in the struggle of the rising capitalist class against the semi-feudal aristocracy of the 16th to 19th centuries. Human beings made capitalism. Human beings can unmake it. But it will not happen automatically: it will require conscious mass struggle.

Lenin said that there was no crisis the ruling class could not survive provided the working class was prepared to pay the price. This is no longer true. The modern crisis of the virus, the climate, and the economy could deliver an uninhabitable world and the destruction of human civilisation. The ruling class may be blind-sided by its vested interest in the system; it may indulge in fantasies about safe 'green zones'; but the truth is that every human-being is under threat.

In the movie *Elysium*, the capitalist class creates an artificial moon circling the Earth, to which they can escape from the social and ecological nightmare below. Such an option is not available to the capitalist class in the real world.

The deepening crisis has been marked by an enormous polarisation of political life. Especially since the 2008 economic crisis, rebel movements have mushroomed.

The Arab Spring brought millions onto the streets to challenge dictatorial regimes and overthrow the hated Mubarak dictatorship in Egypt. Savage austerity in Greece was met by repeated general strikes and pitched battles with the police in Athens and elsewhere. The Occupy! movement started in the US when protestors took their battle to the world's premier financial centre on Wall Street and then went global. In Britain, anti-austerity protests were massive and notable for an uprising of school and university students over fee increases. And in Spain the millions-strong movement of the *Indignados* occupied city squares across the country.

This generalised upsurge was paralleled by left-wing movements taking power in a number of countries in Latin America – the so-called 'Pink Tide' in Venezuela, Brazil, Bolivia, and Ecuador. The left-wing Syriza party in Greece won elections to become the government. And a new left party, *Podemos!*, emerged in Spain with mass support. Soon after, in 2015, Jeremy Corbyn won the leadership of the Labour Party with a massive majority.

In 2020, however, the landscape looks very different. The Arab Spring has been drowned in blood, with tragic consequences, especially in Syria and Egypt. Left-wing governments in Latin America have been overthrown, with the sole exception of Venezuela, and even here there is a deep crisis. The Syriza government capitulated to EU demands for brutal austerity in return for more bailout loans in Greece.

Sections of the capitalist class have unleashed a tidal wave of nationalism and anti-migrant racism designed to head off the Left. This has been coupled with intensified police repression, and has enabled a rapid growth of street fascism.

How should the Left orientate itself in this new situation?

There are three interlinked issues to be confronted: we have to defeat the nationalism, racism, and fascism of the Far Right; we have to learn the lessons of defeats over the last decade and develop new strategies for the Left; and we must clarify the tasks ahead, both immediate challenges and longer-term goals.

All these issues raise the question of *power* – how the capitalist class exercises power, how the working class and the oppressed can confront that power, and how we, the people, can develop a countervailing power of our own capable of moving the world away from the abyss and towards a different future.

Power and the state

The Italian Communist theoretician Antonio Gramsci adopted the term 'hegemony' to describe the domination of the capitalist class. His concept of hegemony highlighted the two key aspects of capitalist rule – repression and ideology, force and fraud.

The capitalist state deploys force – the police, the army, the courts, the prisons – to repress revolt from below and maintain the status quo. In the last decade, state repression has been deployed in bucket-loads against rebel movements – most tragically, perhaps, in Egypt and Syria, where peoples' uprisings were drowned in blood.

But the mechanisms of repression do not just target political protest movements; they are also used to enforce the structures of capitalist power and its attendant social-ideological apparatuses – racism, sexism, other forms of oppression, and the segmentation of spaces by class and ethnicity.

Mike Davis, in his book on Los Angeles in the 1960s, shows how the local police, the LAPD, enforced whites-only housing estates by victimising Black people who tried to buy houses in 'white' areas. In fact, the police enforced curfews against Black people in hundreds of US cities and towns as late as the 1960s. Even now, policing can be brutal in Black, Latino, North African, and other Minority Ethnic districts, not only in the States, but in many other advanced capitalist countries. The police are also available to repress 'unruly' or 'deviant' behaviour threatening to the social order – anything from truancy to minority sexual and gender identities.

During 2020 the American state responded to the Black Lives Matter movement with tear gas, rubber bullets, and armoured cars. At the time of writing, Donald Trump had sent gangs of federal agents to Portland, Oregon, to attack Black Lives Matter protestors. Any idea that the capitalist state is somehow 'neutral' can be tested right now, on the streets, whenever radical movements mobilise against injustice and oppression. Time and again throughout history, when the ruling class loses control, or fears it might, it resorts to violent repression.

But even the least sophisticated capitalist leaders understand that repression on its own is not enough. If ruling elites lose the confidence of most of society, the biggest armies in the world may not save them. They are liable to be overwhelmed by revolution from below as their armies – made up of real people – dissolve into the popular movement.

That is why they combine repression with ideological manipulation. The Nazi Party did not come to power in Germany in 1933 because of the ultra-violence of its Brownshirt street-fighters, but because it had built a mass political base, especially among middle-class people whose lives had been wrecked by the economic crisis, and among the desperate legions of the unemployed. That political base was built on a foundation of German nationalism and antisemitic racism.

World leaders today combine police repression with reactionary ideology: this is the defensive wall around continuing class rule. More and more, as the crisis deepens, ruling-class ideology takes the form of nationalism, racism, and xenophobia – with the alien 'other' demonised as scrounging, predatory, fanatical, undemocratic, crypto-terrorist, and so on.

If the capitalist state acts as the central focus for repression, it also acts as a relay for reactionary ideology. It could not do that effectively without the extraordinary power of today's mass and social media. Fox News was the main TV mouthpiece of Trump in the United States. His Twitter feed reached 80 million people. Facebook is awash with far-right conspiracy theories.

In Britain, BBC news coverage is increasingly craven in the face of Tory threats to the licence fee, sales of Tory rags like the *Daily Mail* and the *Daily Express* dwarf the sales of serious newspapers, while most social-media content is a drip-feed of trivia about celebrities, crime, and consumerism.

Pro-capitalist ideology is also relayed by employers and corporations, by schools and colleges, by religious and recreational institutions, and by families and peer groups. A competitive, consumer-oriented, fashion-conscious individualism focused on 'getting on' and 'not missing out' is a recurring subliminal message percolating through every pore of capitalist society. As Marx said, the dominant ideas of any epoch are the ideas of the ruling class.

The battle of ideas

But this is a culture war that the ruling class must wage with relentless determination if their soporific ideology is to maintain its grip on people's minds. One of the extraordinary consequences of the campaign of social-democrat Bernie Sanders to become the Democratic Party's presidential candidate has been the huge increase in the number of people in the United States who have a favourable view of socialism. Gallup reported in 2019 that four in ten Americans had a positive view of socialism – which, given the wall-to-wall reaction in the US media, is an amazing figure. It demonstrates the importance of mass campaigning, electoral intervention, and having recognised public spokespeople to challenge pro-capitalist propaganda.

Radical change is impossible without a battle of ideas. That has to bring together two things. First, raising anti-capitalist ideas in struggles in the workplace, unions, communities, and radical movements. Second, developing radical media as an alternative to the corporate media. Socialist papers, campaign bulletins, union posters, and agitational leaflets all help, but a left-wing presence on the internet and social media has much wider reach and is now much more important.

Social media are subject to rampant corporate manipulation. They are highly atomising and alienating forms of communication. They are addictive and malignant. But we have no choice but to use the means of communication available to project an alternative socialist message – otherwise we will be voices in the void.

Free speech for democratic and radical ideas has to be defended. It is no accident that Donald Trump made threatening noises about social-media content. He did not have racist and far-right content in mind, but that of radical critics.

In his book *Can Democracy Survive Capitalism?*, Robert Kuttner argues that 'democratic capitalism is today a contradiction in terms'. Empirical reality bears this out. Everywhere, democracy and democratic rights are under attack.

In Britain, the democratic rights of trade unionists and immigrants are severely constrained. In the United States, the right to protest comes under police attack. In the Philippines, the murderous regime of Roberto Duterte has carried out the judicial execution of tens of thousands of alleged drug-dealers. In Turkey, more than a hundred thousand opponents of the Erdoğan government have lost their jobs or been thrown in jail. In Syria, the degenerate regime of Bashar al-Assad, supported by his Russian and Iranian allies, have killed hundreds of thousands of civilians to stay in power. In today's conditions of rising authoritarianism and repression – of what William I Robinson calls a 'Global Police State' – the defence of democracy and basic human rights is a central task for the Left .

Power and the working class

Some people argue that because the old industrial working class has disappeared, socialism is now impossible. The class that socialism is supposed to represent has disappeared. This is false.

First, the working class was always more diverse than just 'industrial' workers. The key criterion for being in the working class is exploitation by capital, not working at a lathe or on a production line. Today, much industrial production – though far from all – has moved from the Global North to the Global South. Key centres of the industrial working class are now in China, Indonesia, Brazil, and Mexico – as well as in the older established economies of the Global North.

In countries like Britain, work has changed profoundly. Millions work in the service sector, banking, the hospitality sector, and retail and personal services. The biggest single employer is the NHS, while hundreds of thousands work in education.

Work has become much more insecure, with millions on zero-hours contracts or in short-term, part-time work. All this leads to a much more differentiated and stratified working class, with those at the top earning four or five times as much as those at the bottom. Many workers are now employed in small enterprises, in contrast to the more concentrated and homogeneous working class of the factory era. There is also a much higher proportion of female and ethnic-minority workers.

A diverse working class creates difficulties for trade unions. A less permanent workforce is harder to organise. So is a workforce dispersed across many small enterprises (to say nothing of the growing numbers working from home in the context of the pandemic). Employers feel much more confident about banning unions and sacking organisers.

But unions can be still be built, and new forms of workforce struggle developed. One example is the targeting of customer interfaces during disputes in the fast-food sector, with workers and their supporters picketing high-street premises and calling on customers to show solidarity by boycotting strike-bound businesses

Equally, as profit-making swivels from production to consumption, struggles over rents and housing – and gentrification and corporate control of the urban landscape more generally – become more important. These are just as much working-class struggles as workplace disputes.

The working class remains the overwhelming majority of society in the developed capitalist economies of the Global North. It has not diminished in size; it has merely changed its form. And more broadly, with the spread of transnational corporate capital across the Global South, the international working class is bigger than ever before, now forming the overwhelming majority of humanity.

Old working-class communities have been smashed up by neoliberalism. New working-class communities are being ravaged by hyper-exploitation. But the closure of mines, shipyards, and factories in the North, and the creation of new types of mega-sweatshop in the South, does not mean the end of the working class; it means a new phase in the development of the class with the capacity to destroy the system that exploits it. But realising that potential will require new forms of organisation and struggle, and winning a new generation to the idea of revolution and socialist transformation.

Parties and movements

Radical rebellion against neoliberalism expresses itself in workers' and community struggles, and in mass protest movements. The question is how these struggles and movements can be fused into a global fight for an alternative future at both the national and international level.

What happens when one particular struggle is over, or a protest movement goes into decline? With the mass movements against austerity that emerged after 2008, like the *Indignados* in Spain and Occupy! in the United States, the answer is clear. As struggles mount, people seek a political force at a national level to represent them. The *Indignados* movement was the mass base for the establishment of *Podemos!* ('We Can'), and the Occupy! movement led to the trend inside the US Democratic Party around Bernie Sanders that called itself 'Our Revolution' – heavily staffed and influenced by the Democratic Socialists of America.

These movements – and others like them – had their pluses and minuses. But they failed to break through. It seems that capitalism could not be overthrown by an electoral alliance of social-democrats and revolutionaries. Why not? Why do the working class and the oppressed need a revolutionary party of their own? This issue was addressed by the veteran French revolutionary Daniel Bensaïd in the following way:

> *From a certain point of view, capitalism will indeed be overthrown by an alliance, or a convergence, of mass social movements. But even if these movements, because of their liberatory projects, perceive capitalism to be their enemy (which perhaps is the case for the women's movement or the environmental movement, not just the workers' movement), I don't think these movements all play an equivalent role. And all are traversed by differences and contradictions which reflect their position, in the face of capital as a global mode of domination.*

> *There is a 'naturalist' feminism and a revolutionary feminism, a profoundly anti-humanist environmentalism and a humanist and social environmentalism… If you consider these arenas are… simply juxtaposed, then perhaps you could devise a tactic of putting together changing coalitions ('rainbow coalitions' on immediate questions). But there would be no solid strategic convergence in such an approach.*

> *I think, on the contrary, that within a particular mode of production (capitalism), relations of exploitation and class conflict constitute an overarching framework which cuts across and unifies the other contradictions. Capital itself is the great unifier which subordinates every aspect of social production and reproduction, remodelling the function of the family, determining the social division of labour, and submitting humanity's conditions of social reproduction to the law of value. If that is indeed the case, a party, and not simply the sum of social movements, is the best agent of conscious unification.*

We agree with Bensaïd's outlook here. The political party remains what Gramsci called 'The Modern Prince' (a reference to Machiavelli's idealised Renaissance prince in his book of that name, where the ruling prince is conceived as the primary agent of the public good). The prince/party becomes the means whereby the demands and struggles of the exploited and the oppressed can be unified and synthesised in an overall strategic project for taking power.

Socialists are the best fighters for even partial gains for the working class, and they always operate as activists embedded in the mass struggles and campaigns of the oppressed. But they need to operate with the long-term aim of uniting the struggles and campaigns, which means building a socialist party – not a sect or propaganda group interested only in recruiting a few more members, but a broad party of working-class activists, where diverse outlooks are embraced, and political differences are debated.

Neoliberalism since the mid-1980s has shown that the Far Right, despite its anti-state rhetoric, relies on control of government and the state apparatus to push through its agenda. Workers and popular campaigns fight back, but unless the forces of resistance are brought together in a united anti-capitalist movement at a national level, they will be incapable of contesting for power. If a national anti-capitalist movement is built, democratically organised from the bottom up, with its own programme for social transformation, with a clear strategy for waging mass struggle, then it is effectively a political party, whatever it might call itself.

But it is a recurring dilemma of protest and resistance movements that mass struggles – strikes, demonstrations, sit-ins, occupations, and so on – do not lead to lasting gains unless alternative power structures emerge capable of challenging capital and the state at a national level. Without such an outcome, protest and resistance can be demobilised, absorbed back into the system, or, if necessary, crushed by violent force.

Radical governments can be assessed by two criteria: what actions do they take to promote the interests and struggles of the working class and the poor; and what is the relationship between the government and the mass movement.

Failed projects: 1. Brazil, Venezuela, and Bolivia

Key experiences here are the left-wing governments of the last two decades in Brazil, Venezuela, and Bolivia – the Workers Party (PT) government in Brazil, the 'Chavista' and 'Bolivarian' government in Venezuela, and the MAS (Movement towards Socialism) government of Evo Morales in Bolivia.

Each of these experiences involved years of struggle and conflict, with the capitalist class and the Right, but also within the Left. The Brazilian PT government was overthrown by a parliamentary-judicial coup in 2016. Evo Morales was overthrown by a military coup in 2019, and has only recently been able to return to the country. The 'Chavista' government in Venezuela – named after its founder and main leader, the late Hugo Chavez – is still in power, but in a situation of dire economic crisis, collapsing popular support, and under siege from both inside and outside the country. How are we to explain the limited and contested achievements of this popular wave?

The hostility of the Right, the capitalist class, and significant sections of the middle class – with financial and political support from the US – has been an enduring feature of all three of these governments. But that does not explain the drift towards the economic crisis and falling popular support which allowed them to be overthrown or destabilised. To understand that it is necessary to look at the political strategy of each government.

All three governments operated on the basis of what Jeffery R Webber calls 'extractive reformism'. The basic idea was to maximise the tax revenues from the export of oil (Venezuela and Brazil), tin and other minerals (Bolivia), and agricultural products like soya beans (Brazil). The tax revenues would then be used to help the poorest in society, without having to dispossess the capitalist class and its wealthy allies.

In the years up to the 2008 world economic crisis, this strategy worked. Global economic expansion, particularly of the Chinese economy, generated massive demand for exports of primary commodities like oil, minerals, and foodstuffs. But after the crash, the attempt at income redistribution through extractive reformism collapsed – and with it, much of the mass support these governments had enjoyed.

The strategic choice had been whether or not to mobilise the masses for a head-on collision with the capitalist class, with the aim of taking power not just at a governmental level, but at every level of society, in order to effect its complete transformation. The Brazilian, Venezuelan, and Bolivian left governments refused do this – and thereby condemned themselves to eventual defeat when boom turned to bust in the world's commodity markets.

Failed projects: 2. Corbynism

For the Left in Europe, huge hopes invested in the Syriza government in Greece, *Podemos!* in Spain, and of course the Corbyn leadership in the British Labour Party. All these projects reflect key political weaknesses of different variants of *reformism*.

Who brought down Jeremy Corbyn? Corbynism had enemies on the Right in Britain and internationally, of course, but its overthrow would not have been possible without the Labour Right, especially in parliament and at the top of some of the trade unions. They were never reconciled to a left leadership, and did everything possible to overthrow it, using whatever means came to hand. Because, after all, they are politicians and officials embedded in the system, representatives of the status quo, albeit a more liberal version than that of the Tories.

This was never fully grasped by many Corbyn supporters, including a good number at the highest level. In reality, it was always literally incredible to imagine a radical left-reformist programme, with many measures against the immediate interests of British and international capital, being implemented by a parliamentary party dead-set against it.

The weakness of the Corbynistas at the parliamentary level was overwhelming. It could be seen in the composition of the various incarnations of the Shadow Cabinet. Corbyn was compelled to recruit people like Keir Starmer, Emily Thornberry, and others who never shared his politics. At times, Corbyn had difficulty getting a Shadow Cabinet together at all.

The only way that a radical-left programme could have been forced through the PLP (Parliamentary Labour Party) would have been by altering the composition of that body – that is, by unleashing a country-wide mandatory re-selection campaign and hurling the entire party, at every level, into a ferocious civil war.

Without this, the Corbyn leadership was a prisoner of the Labour Right. Perhaps the clearest measure of this was its pitiful failure to stand up to the relentless barrage of accusations that Corbyn and his supporters were antisemitic. The core of these accusations was a false equation between antisemitism and anti-Zionism. But instead of taking a principled stand against racism, imperialism, and the dispossession of the Palestinian people – and therefore against Zionism – the Labour leadership simply rolled over.

The leadership's position on Brexit was also shambolic. Instead of recognising the rotten core of nationalism and racism at the heart of Brexit – instead of seeing it for what it was, the banner of the Tory Right, UKIP/ the Brexit Party, and the fascists – Corbyn attempted to 'triangulate' with (progressive) Remain and (reactionary) Leave voters. Again, this ideological flinching allowed the Right to win further ground (and ultimately to take the Tory leadership and the general election).

A brilliant opportunity was lost, with a force of perhaps 40,000-plus Momentum members, to push back and isolate the PLP Right, and to turn the Labour Party into a mass campaigning organisation focused on struggle and resistance. It was an opportunity spurned because the Corbyn leadership harboured the notion that a compromise could be reached with the Right that would allow the radical-left project to go ahead, without a showdown fight.

Corbynism could only have withstood the onslaught if its leadership and base had been more organised, orientated to mass mobilisation and fighting the Labour Right, and more ideologically hardened. That would have been something different from Corbynism.

Failed projects: 3. Syriza and *Podemos!*
Syriza (the Coalition of the Radical Left) won the 2014 general election in Greece, with its leader Alexis Tsipras becoming Prime Minister. *Podemos!* joined the Socialist Party government in Spain in 2020, with its leader Pablo Iglesias becoming deputy Primer Minister.

After six months in office, Syriza agreed to a savage austerity package imposed by the 'Troika' of European Commission, European Central Bank, and International Monetary Fund – even after the Greek people had voted the package down in a referendum! This plunged Greece into social collapse and started a plunge in Syriza's mass support that ended in electoral rout.

Podemos! is currently providing left cover for the austerity programme of Spain's Socialist government, causing its radical wing, the *Anticapitalistas*, to break away.

In both cases, prolonged mass struggles have been led down a blind alley. Both the right-wing of Syriza and the leadership of *Podemos!* have their origins in 1970s 'Eurocommunism' – essentially a variant of social-dem-ocratic reformism. They shared the illusion that tactical manoeuvring would enable them to make progressive changes without tackling capitalist power.

The Left in both Greece and Spain, and more widely in Europe and the world, has to learn the lessons of these defeats: crucially, that becom-ing the government without mobilising the working class and oppressed to take control of society means eventual capitulation and defeat.

Failed projects: 4. Argentina's *piqueteros*

A classic example of mass resistance with a disappointing outcome was what happened in Argentina in 2001-3. Little known on the British Left, the turn-of-century crisis in Argentina gave rise to some of the most advanced form of mass self-organisation, workers' control, and workers' self-man-agement seen anywhere in the world in the last 80 years.

In July 2001, the government of Fernando de la Rua responded to an economic crisis by cutting civil servants pay by 13% and savaging social welfare. In December that year, as the crisis worsened, the government stopped all cash withdrawals from banks.

The economic collapse was on a scale not witnessed again until the Covid-19 crisis. Millions of people lost their jobs, their pensions, and their savings. The response was a mass uprising on 19 December, around the slogan ¡Que se vayan todos! ('Kick them all out!')

In the face of social catastrophe, local assemblies emerged every-where, in both working-class and middle-class areas, which both coordi-nated protest action, but also attempted to take over the running of local economic life and welfare services. This included re-starting production in closed-down shops, bakeries, workshops, and small factories, organising food production and distribution, and trying to negotiate subsidies from national and local government. It was later estimated that a third of the Argentinian population had participated in the assemblies.

Overlapping these local action committees was the movement of the unemployed, the *piqueteros* ('pickets'), so called because of their tactic of occupying and closing down major highways.

Inside the movement of the unemployed, a multitude of different, conflicting, and sometimes overlapping trends emerged. Eventually they coalesced into three major groups. The dominant trend, the *Movimiento de Trabajadores Desocupados* – Unemployed Workers Movement (MTD) – argued that the way forward was to build the counter-power of the work-ing class and the oppressed, to take the form of self-managed produc-tion and local social organisation, separate from and against the capitalist economy and state. The MTD set up a network of productive workshops and enterprises, like local construction teams and self-sustaining neigh-bourhood bakeries, in an effort to become independent from aid and instead rely on their own alternative system.

They argued against any strategy of trying to take state power and establish a national government of the working class. The two minority currents of the *piqueteros*, the Class Combat Current (CCC) and the Federation of Workers for the Land, Housing, and Habitat (FTV), tended to put more emphasis on gaining concessions from the government.

Two things happened that disabled the main MTD strategy and moved the situation to the restoration of capitalist 'normality'. First, the movement for the self-organised and independent economy ran out of steam. Lacking capital and raw materials, few workshops and small factories could stay open under workers' self-management. A regime of workers' control and self-organisation can survive only for a limited time without an advance to an alternative social system at a national level. The counter-power of the working class and the oppressed could not be sustained without conquering the state and exercising control over major levers of the economy.

Second, the *piqueteros*, as the organisations negotiating with local and national government about subsidies to finance public works and give people at least part-time jobs, became a sort of job-allocation bureaucracy. Its radical charge became dissipated.

Crisis is the test of politics. In Argentina there was an extraordinary economic and political crisis, an extreme social collapse, and a tremendous upsurge of struggle, organisation, and self-activity from below.

But there was no prior organisation of revolutionary forces and no network of activists embedded in the popular movements with a clear vision of social transformation and a clear strategy for achieving it. The Argentinian workers did not even have their own independent mass social-democratic party. The post-2001 crisis was an historic opportunity for anti-capitalist social change, but one that failed for lack of political leadership.

The fundamental strategic issue: can we change the world without taking power?

The central question is whether in order to achieve system change – to create a green, feminist, anti-racist, egalitarian, non-violent, and democratic society – we have to take state power. The answer is yes.

Such a revolutionary perspective – where the self-activity of the working class and the oppressed is linked to a new type of anti-capitalist government – has always been resisted by reformists, whether traditional social-democrats, Eurocommunists, or a mixture of both.

Some have argued that creating a left-wing government is in itself dangerous, leading only to new forms of authoritarianism. John Holloway, an academic working in Mexico, wrote a book in 2002 called *Change the World without Taking Power*. He argues that the struggle between the people on one side and the rich and powerful on the other goes on eternally and we have to continue to fight back on a daily basis. But, he says, we should not have the ambition of taking state power, because a state representing the workers and the oppressed is bound to be authoritarian and repressive.

There are so many problems with Holloway's argument. One is that if we try to ignore the capitalist state, it certainly will not ignore us, especially when the Left and radical movements become powerful. The capitalist class will use their police, their army, their propaganda machine in the media, as well as fascist and other far-right movements – everything they have – to defeat us.

In these circumstances, people in struggle are bound to organise for their own defence – against scabs, the police, and fascist mobs. This is precisely what happened when the recent Black Lives Matter protests came under attack in the States. As this happens, people begin to create new forms of participatory democracy and community-based networks. If the struggle intensifies, these can swell into a national network – a new kind of popular power – an alternative state – the embryo of a government of the workers and the oppressed.

This has happened again and again in revolutionary situations – in England in the 1640s, in Paris in the 1790s, in Paris again in 1871, in Petrograd in 1917, in Munich and Budapest in 1919, in Barcelona in 1936, in Budapest again in 1956, in Iran in 1979, and so many other places at so many other times. This happens irrespective of whether theorists like John Holloway think it is a good idea: it happens because the logic of the struggle makes it necessary.

And the truth is that all these experiments in revolutionary democracy are the precise opposite of 'authoritarian' and 'repressive'. The record shows them to have been the highest forms of democracy – moments when the largest possible number of ordinary people, including the poorest, the most oppressed and marginalised, come onto the stage of history poised to play their part in its remaking.

That is why revolutions from below are smashed with such violence; it is because the ruling classes of the world are chilled to the bone by the threat of mass democracy that they will sometimes murder tens of thousands in their rampages of counter-revolutionary terror.

Knowing that – armed with the bitter lessons of history – we cannot duck the central strategic question: the workers and the oppressed, to liberate humanity and save the planet, must overthrow the state, dispossess the capitalist class, assume full governmental authority, and set about the essential world-historical task of building a new social order

Conclusion

The Revolutionary Imperative

Covid-19 is a disease of capitalism. Penetration of the wilderness on the frontiers of global capital accumulation has destroyed natural firebreaks. Viruses have entered the human food-chain and evolved new and more lethal forms. Agribusiness complexes and slum mega-cities have acted as incubators. Modern communications networks have ensured rapid spread. Neoliberal regimes have spent decades hollowing out public-health provision and outsourcing services to corporate profiteers. The result is a lethal pandemic and an economic disaster.

The pandemic is one facet of capitalism's rupture with Nature. There are so many more: the toxins being pumped into the Earth's water systems; the trillions of tiny particles of plastic in foodstuffs; the poisoning of the air in the mega-cities where most of us live; the destruction of natural habitats and the fast-unfolding 'sixth mass extinction'; the loading of the atmosphere with carbon waste, the overheating of the Earth, and the accelerating collapse of the global ecosystems on which we all depend.

This 'metabolic rift' is a direct consequence of capitalism: a system of unplanned, unregulated, globalised capital accumulation in the interests of profit, corporate power, and the super-rich. This system is predatory and insatiable. It is responsible not only for ecological devastation, but also for social collapse.

Inequalities, both within and between states, have soared in the 40 years of the neoliberal era. The gap between rich and poor has never been wider. Only a third of the world's people are in secure jobs. The rest are precarious or surplus, the majority now living in mega slum-cities, some working in low-paid casual jobs, some in the informal economy, some displaced and destitute.

The demolition of welfare states in the Global North and the evisceration of national-development programmes in the Global South have deepened the anguish at the base of society. An ever more lopsided social order makes 1% obscenely rich, pampers and privileges another 15% – a middle class of functionaries in service to the system – and leaves the rest, the working class, facing increasingly precarious work, stagnant or falling living standards, disintegrating public services, and a growing sense of social decay and a darkening future.

The breakdown in the old 'welfare consensus' creates a crisis of legitimacy for the system – and the response is nationalism and racism to divide the working class, and militarised police repression to crush the resistance of those who fight back. That is why the shadow of fascism now looms over the world again.

The root cause of the crisis runs deep. Stretching back half a century or more, capitalism has been afflicted by an insoluble problem of 'over-accumulation' – too much surplus capital seeking profitable investment in clogged-up markets where workers do not earn enough to buy back the products of their own labour ('under-consumption'). This explains the many pathologies of neoliberal economics: financialisation, speculation, and permanent debt; the waste of the military-industrial-security complex; the plundering of the commons, the profiting from privatisation, outsourcing, and state contracts; the laying waste of Nature; the sucking of all humanity into a vortex of sweat-shop exploitation and manic consumption.

It is the greatest crisis in human history. We are hurtling towards the abyss. The system is terminally diseased. Capital came into the world, Marx wrote, 'dripping from head to toe, from every pore, with blood and dirt'. Now, the ageing system is putrescent and gangrenous.

It is time to end it – time to terminate the 500-year reign of capital, time to overthrow the militarised states that uphold it. This means organising and mobilising the potentially transformative power of the international working class – the vast majority of us, women and men, black and white, young and old, gay and straight, disabled and able-bodied.

When the exploited and oppressed move into action, when the masses united come onto the stage of history, the Earth shakes. It happened in 1789, 1917, 1968, and 1989. It happened with the Suffragettes and the Civil Rights Movement; with the anti-globalisation and anti-war movements; with the Arab Spring, the school climate strikes, and the Black Lives Matter insurgency.

The world is ever more polarised. On one side stand the super-rich, the corporations, the middle class, the police, the fascists. On the other stand the workers, the oppressed, the poor, the wretched of the earth. They are few, we are many. That is why they need lies to divide us, as well as cops to bludgeon us, if they are to maintain their rule.

Their power is immense. It is the power of corporate capital and the militarised states combined. It is the greatest concentration of power the world has ever seen. But, also, the global working class is bigger than ever before, and if mobilised in all its strength, it could bring the system down.

This alternative future is possible. But everything depends on politics. The growing scale and speed of the crisis will make a mockery of any programme of piecemeal reform. We have, in any case, seen a succession of reformist projects crash over the last decade: the Workers Party in Brazil, the MAS in Bolivia, the Chavistas in Venezuela; Syriza in Greece and *Podemos!* in Spain; the movements around Corbyn in Britain and Sanders in the United States.

We have also been witness to the failure of identity politics and autonomist organisation. The politics of difference and separation does not lead to 'empowerment', but to fragmentation, weakness, and easy containment by the forces of capital and the state. A plethora of small, local, independent campaigns that never co-ordinate, never combine, never become a mass movement is not an alternative strategy for social transformation: it is no strategy at all.

Capital and the state are highly centralised. Only a concentrated power can have any hope of defeating them. The fate of the Argentinian *piqueteros* provides a sharp lesson: a powerful mass movement from below is not enough in itself; it must be welded into a political force capable of taking control of the workplaces and overthrowing the state.

If there is mass resistance from below – strikes, blockades, occupations, demonstrations. If these swell and fuse into a united popular movement. If new organs of participatory democracy, of people power, emerge at the base and assume control over workplaces and communities. If these things happen, consciousness will grow, confidence surge, and ordinary human beings will discover that they do not need to remain cogs in the capitalist machine, but, collectively, can take control over their own lives. The name for this is socialism.

To achieve it, to weld ten thousand campaigns and struggles into one, to turn a world of discontent and resistance into a single mass movement strong enough to win, we need unity and organisation; we need a channelling of energy into a single tidal wave of transformative popular power. We need – whatever form it takes – a revolutionary party.

Capital and the state will threaten ferocious violence. They will be willing to drown the movement in blood, as they have done so many times in the past. So the movement must dispossess the capitalist class and overthrow the capitalist state. The name for this is revolution.

We, the authors of this book, are revolutionary socialists. We believe that the old order is doomed and we must build a new one based on democracy, internationalism, ecosocialism, solidarity with the poor and the oppressed, and the total transformation of society to serve human need not private greed.

That is the task facing humanity in the third decade of the 21st century. That is what we must do if we are to save ourselves and our planet. That is the revolutionary imperative.

Suggested Further Reading

This reading list has two functions. First, in the absence of formal academic referencing, it gives some indication of the studies on which we have drawn, and this is an indication of some of our wider affinities. Second, it recommends a range of further reading. To help readers select other works to read, while articles/books are listed in author and date order, chapters for which they are especially relevant are given in brackets. Online versions can be found of some of these texts. Many others are obtainable in cheap second-hand editions.

Anonymous, 2020, Marxism and Transgender Liberation:confronting transphobia on the British Left, London, Red Fightback. (9)

Baldwin, J, 1955, *Notes of a Native Son*, Boston, Beacon Press. (9)

Baran, P and Sweezy, P, 1966, *Monopoly Capital: an essay on the American economic and social order*, New York, Monthly Review Press. (7)

Callinicos, A, 1983, *The Revolutionary Ideas of Karl Marx*, London, Bookmarks.

Cliff, T, 1988, *The Labour Party: a Marxist analysis*, London, Bookmarks. (8)

Davis, M, 2006, *Planet of Slums*, London, Verso. (4)

Davis, M, 2020, *The Monster Enters: Covid-19, Avian Flu, and the plagues of capitalism*, New York, O/R Books. (1)

Denvir, D, 2020, *All-American Nativism: how the bipartisan war on immigrants explains politics as we know it*, London, Verso. (5, 6, 9)

Dunayevskaya, R, 1958, *Marxism and Freedom: from 1776 until today*, New York, Humanity Books.

Faulkner, N, 2017, *A People's History of the Russian Revolution*, London, Pluto. (10)

Faulkner, N, 2018, *A Radical History of the World*, London, Pluto.

Faulkner, N, Dathi, S, Hearse, P, and Syeda, S, 2019, *Creeping Fascism: what it is and how to fight it*, London, Public Reading Rooms. (6)

Fekete, L, 2009, *A Suitable Enemy: racism, migration, and Islamophobia in Europe*, London, Pluto. (6, 9)

Fekete, L, 2018, *Europe's Fault Lines: racism and the rise of the Right*, London, Verso. (6)

Foster, J B, 2002, *Ecology Against Capitalism*, New York, Monthly Review Press. (2)

Foster, J B, 2009, *The Financial Crisis: causes and consequences*, New York, Monthly Review Press. (7)

Foster, J B and McChesney, R W, 2012, *The Endless Crisis: how monopoly-finance capital produces stagnation and upheaval from the USA to China*, New York, Monthly Review Press. (7)

Foster, J B, 2017, *Trump in the White House: tragedy and farce*, New York, Monthly Review Press. (6)

Freire, P,1970, *Pedagogy of the Oppressed*, London, The Left Book Club. (9)

Haider, A, 2018, *Mistaken Identity: race and class in the age of Trump*, London, Verso. (9)

Hannah, S, 2018, *A Party with Socialists in it: a history of the Labour Left*, London, Pluto. (8)

Lenin, V I, 1916, *Imperialism: the highest stage of capitalism*, www.marxists.org (7)

Lenin, V I, 1917, *State and Revolution*, www.marxists.org (10)

Luxemburg, R, 2008, *The Essential Rosa Luxemburg*, Chicago, Haymarket.

Malm, A, 2016, *Fossil Capital*, London, Verso. (2)

Mandel, E, 1967, *An Introduction to Marxist Economic Theory*, www.marxists.org (7)

Mandel, E, 1982, *An Introduction to Marxism*, London, Pluto.

Marx, K, 1871, *The Civil War in France*, www.marxists.org (10)

Miliband, R, 1961, *Parliamentary Socialism: a study in the politics of Labour*, London, Allen & Unwin. (8)

Miliband, R, 1973, *The State in Capitalist Society*, London, Quartet. (5, 10)

Molyneux, J, 1978, *Marxism and the Party*, London, Pluto. (10)

Neale, J, 2008, *Stop Global Warming: change the world*, London, Bookmarks. (2)

Robinson, W I, 2004, *A Theory of Global Capitalism: production, class, and state in a transnational world*, Baltimore, John Hopkins University. (7)

Robinson, W I , 2014, *Global Capitalism and the Crisis of Humanity*, Cambridge, Cambridge University Press. (3, 4, 7)

Robinson, W I, 2020, *The Global Police State*, London, Pluto. (5, 6, 7)

Rowbotham, S, 1972, *Women, Resistance, and Revolution*, Harmondsworth, Penguin. (9)

Rowbotham, S, 1973, *Woman's Consciousness, Man's World*, Harmondsworth, Penguin. (9)

Thornett, A, 2019, *Facing the Apocalypse: arguments for ecosocialism*, London, Resistance Books. (2)

Trotsky, L, 1971, *The Struggle Against Fascism in Germany*, New York, Pathfinder. (6)

Wallace, R, 2016, *Big Farms Make Big Flu: dispatches on infectious disease, agribusiness, and the nature of science*, New York, Monthly Review Press. (1)

Wallace, R, 2020, Dead Epidemiologists: on the origins of Covid-19, New York, Monthly Review Press. (1)

Wallace-Wells, D, 2019, *The Uninhabitable Earth: a story of the future*, London, Penguin. (2)

Williams-Findley, B, 2020, *More than a Left Foot*, London, Resistance Books. (9)

The Authors

Neil Faulkner is an archaeologist, historian, and political activist. His books include *Rome: empire of the eagles*, *A Radical History of the World*, *A People's History of the Russian Revolution*, and *Creeping Fascism: what it is and how to fight it*. He is currently working on *A People's History of the Spanish Civil War*. His books have been translated into a dozen foreign languages. He played a leading role in Brick Lane Debates and is now active in Anti*Capitalist Resistance.

Phil Hearse is a veteran socialist activist. One of the authors of *Creeping Fascism*, he taught Communication and Culture at a London college until his retirement in 2016. Many of his articles appear on the Socialist Resistance, International Viewpoint, and Mutiny websites. He is a supporter of Anti*Capitalist Resistance.

Nina Fortune is an activist with a focus on oppression. She has contributed essays to *Mutiny* about Black Lives Matter in the US and the disproportionate impact of coronavirus on BAME people in the UK.

Rowan Fortune is a socialist, the editor of the utopian short story anthology *Citizens of Nowhere*, and author of the nonfiction ebook *Writing Nowhere*.

Simon Hannah is a local government worker and a socialist and trade union activist. He is the author of *A Party with Socialists in it: a history of the Labour Left*, *Can't Pay, Won't Pay: the fight to stop the Poll Tax*, and *Radical Lambeth*.

What is Anti*Capitalist Resistance

We are an organisation of revolutionary socialists. We believe red-green revolution is necessary to meet the compound crisis of humanity and the planet.

We are internationalists, ecosocialists, and anti-capitalist revolutionaries. We oppose imperialism, nationalism, and militarism, and all forms of discrimination, oppression, and bigotry. We support the self-organisation of women, Black people, disabled people, and LGBTIQ+ people. We support all oppressed people fighting imperialism and forms of apartheid, and struggling for self-determination, including the people of Palestine.

We favour mass resistance to neoliberal capitalism. We work inside existing mass organisations, but we believe grassroots struggle to be the core of effective resistance, and that the emancipation of the working class and the oppressed will be the act of the working class and the oppressed.

We reject forms of left organisation that focus exclusively on electoralism and social-democratic reforms. We also oppose top-down 'democratic-centralist' models. We favour a pluralist organisation that can learn from struggles at home and across the world.

We aim to build a united organisation rooted in the struggles of the working class and the oppressed, and committed to debate, initiative, and self-activity. We are for social transformation based on mass participatory democracy.

info@anticapitalistresistance.org
www.anticapitalistresistance.org

About the Publishers

RESISTANCE BOOKS is a radical publisher of internationalist, ecosocialist, and feminist books. Resistance Books publishes books in collaboration with the International Institute for Research and Education (iire.org), and the Fourth International (https://fourth.international). For further information, including a full list of titles available and how to order them, go to the Resistance Books website.

Email: info@resistancebooks.org
Website: resistancebooks.org

THE INTERNATIONAL INSTITUTE FOR RESEARCH AND EDUCATION is a centre for the development of critical thought and the exchange of experiences and ideas between people engaged in their struggles. Since 1982, when the Institute opened in Amsterdam, it has organised courses for progressive forces around the world which deal with all subjects related to the emancipation of the oppressed and exploited. The IIRE provides activists and academics opportunities for research and education in three locations: Amsterdam, Islamabad and Manila. The IIRE publishes Notebooks for Study and Research in several languages. They focus on contemporary political debates, as well as themes of historical and theoretical importance.

Email: iire@iire.org
Website: iire.org

Lightning Source UK Ltd.
Milton Keynes UK
UKHW011229180321
380574UK00001B/97